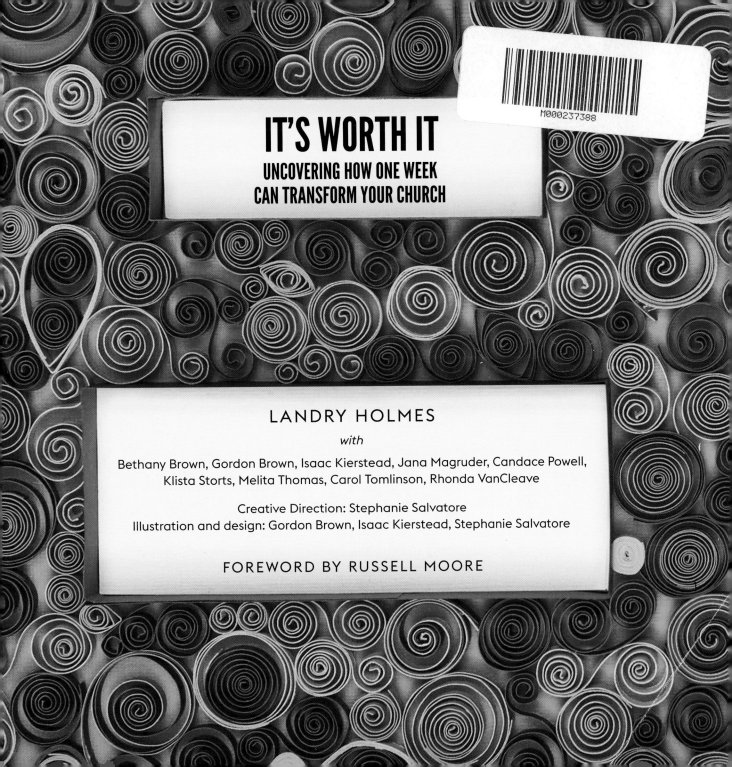

IT'S WORTH IT

UNCOVERING HOW ONE WEEK CAN TRANSFORM YOUR CHURCH

LANDRY HOLMES

with

Bethany Brown, Gordon Brown, Isaac Kierstead, Jana Magruder, Candace Powell, Klista Storts, Melita Thomas, Carol Tomlinson, Rhonda VanCleave

Creative Direction: Stephanie Salvatore
Illustration and design: Gordon Brown, Isaac Kierstead, Stephanie Salvatore

FOREWORD BY RUSSELL MOORE

© 2018 LifeWay Christian Resources.

Item 005814067
ISBN 978-1-5359-5273-6

Published by LifeWay Christian Resources,
One LifeWay Plaza, Nashville, TN 37234

For ordering or inquiries, visit www.lifeway.com,
or write LifeWay Resources Customer Service,
One LifeWay Plaza, Nashville, TN 37234-0113.

We believe that the Bible has God for its author; salvation for its end; and truth, without any mixture of error, for its matter and that all Scripture is totally true and trustworthy. To review LifeWay's doctrinal guideline, please visit lifeway.com/doctrinalguideline.

All Scripture quotations are taken from the Christian Standard Bible® Copyright 2017 by Holman Bible Publishers. Used by permission.

To all VBS leaders and teachers

past, present, and future

who have, continue to, and will

faithfully steward

the message of the gospel.

IT'S WORTH IT!

TABLE OF CONTENTS

3 IT'S WORTH IT ... BECAUSE THE GOSPEL IS PERSONAL

4 IT'S WORTH IT ... BECAUSE ETERNITY IS WORTH IT

ENDNOTES

FOREWORD

This year, at some point, a gathering of influential people will assemble to decide the future of life and culture as we know it. I'm not referring to the Supreme Court or the United Nations. I am not referring to the White House cabinet table or a congressional leadership caucus. I'm referring to Vacation Bible School.

That's because Jesus understood, and understands, something that this social Darwinian fallen world of ours never does—children are more important than the pomp and splendor of what passes for "powerful" and "influential" in this post-Eden universe (Matthew 21:15; Mark 10:13-16).

The ministries of local churches in teaching the Bible to the children of Christian families and communicating the gospel to neighborhood children who have never heard it is among the most important and effective aspects of Christian ministry today. I say that as someone who, I am quite sure, would not be in ministry today if not for Vacation Bible School. I have met numbers of people, too numerous to count, who have a similar story. They were found by Jesus at Vacation Bible School. Or they were called to a ministry there. Or they had their eyes opened to the glory of God in global missions there. Or they learned a Scripture song that embedded in their memories and resurfaced just when they needed it most.

The common factor in all these stories is that these VBS gatherings, so important to so many of us, were not especially "slick" or "cutting edge" or "cool." We marched into my little church for opening assembly every morning not to some market-tested jingle, but to the majestic strains of "Onward, Christian Soldiers." My pastor, who greeted us there was not some "relatable-to-children" communicator. He wore a suit and read from the Bible. That was the genius of it all. We were taken seriously as people who belonged to Christ, or who could belong to Christ, and therefore could be held responsible to know and share the old, old story. We heard about missions as though we were being trained to carry on the Great Commission ourselves, which, of course, we were.

That's why I am thrilled to see this long-needed book go forward. Vacation Bible School is needed now more than ever, at a time when more and more children and their families have no access to the gospel, at a time when biblical illiteracy and missions apathy is widespread even among "churched" populations, much less the general population.

Sometime this year, yet another new generation of children will march into a church building, or maybe a neighborhood park pavilion, or a rented school for Vacation Bible School. They might have different snacks than the flower-shaped butter cookies with the hole in the middle and red Kool-Aid that my peers and I had. They will, no doubt, have different songs and some different games. But they will hear the same gospel from the same Bible. And they'll hear it, as I did, from people who love them, and who picture through that the love of God for them and for the world.

Those children are not just "the future" in the way the world often speaks of such things. They are the future in the sense that those who come to faith in Christ are joint-heirs with Christ and heirs of a new creation, forever (Rom. 8:17). Vacation Bible School, then, at your church, is more important than an international summit of global political leaders or economists or technology entrepreneurs. The devil trembles at that. Jesus is the ultimate King of the cosmos, and He welcomes the little children to join Him. You ask me how I know that?

I learned it in Vacation Bible School.

Russell Moore
President
Ethics & Religious Liberty Commission of the Southern Baptist Convention

INTRODUCTION

The three little letters V-B-S often evoke emotions for many of us because our salvation stories are tied to Vacation Bible School. I am one of those people. I was nine years old at a church in Houston, Texas, when I felt the Holy Spirit tug at my heart after the pastor shared the gospel and asked if any of us wanted to learn more about following Jesus. This was not the first time I had heard the plan of salvation delivered. After all, I was a church kid—and not only that, I was a minister's kid. Our family was at church twice on Sunday and usually more than once during the rest of the week. It was my life. Let's put it this way—this wasn't my first VBS. But, it was my time to respond.

I had recently been feeling more convicted of sin—specifically coveting the outfits of my friends (by the way—the sanctification process is so real as I still struggle!). But, at some point as a little girl I knew it was wrong. I even asked my parents if it was wrong to want the clothes that my friend had and wish she didn't have them. "Yes, it is, Jana. That's called coveting and it is sinful." Their patience to let that sink in and not rush me into a sinner's prayer was wisdom. I needed to sit with the realization of my sin a little longer.

You see, all of the Sunday School lessons, choir lyrics about Jesus, Bible verse memory charts, and previous VBS weeks culminated into a specific time for the Holy Spirit to move in my heart to say, "Yes—I want to know more." My parents were notified and that night they prayed with me to receive Christ. Not too long afterwards, my daddy baptized me. Ever since then, VBS has been part of my testimony.

That was more than 35 years ago and, truthfully, I do not recall many specific memories from that particular week of VBS. I'm sure we did crafts and games, sang songs, recited pledges, and had Kool-Aid and animal crackers for our snack—but I don't remember any of those things. What I DO remember is the Thursday of that week when our pastor came to talk to us about Jesus and how He died for our sin. Even though I knew our pastor (#staffkid), I had never heard him talk to just us kids. It was a big deal for him to walk in the room, look us in the eyes, and share the gospel in a way we could understand. I sat up straight in my chair and I listened—and I wanted to know more. To this day, I am so grateful for Pastor Jerry Lemon who emulates what Charles Spurgeon describes in his book, *Come Ye Children*: "Blessed is he who can so speak as to be understood by a child!"[1]

I do still have my VBS certificates that my mom saved for me. These pieces of paper are special to me because they mark mountaintop experiences in my faith journey that eventually led to the ultimate—a relationship with Jesus. These certificates represent hundreds of adults who gave up a week of their summers to pour into the lives of children. I wish I could find all of those men and women and thank them personally, but I know I can't. However, it is with them in mind and in honor of them—along with Pastor Jerry—that I write this introduction to such an important book.

I am honored to lead the LifeWay Kids team in serving churches all over the world with VBS resources and training each year. We have the privilege of hearing from many of those churches as they report back astounding numbers and stories of how the Lord has used VBS to reach tens of thousands of children, students, and adults with the gospel. Members of that team and I have partnered with our LifeWay Research colleagues to encourage you to uncover the answer to the question, "Is VBS worth it?"

I realize that there are many of you in ministry who might be at a place where you are asking if VBS is still worth it. After all, it takes an army of volunteers, a chunk of your budget, and an endless supply of energy and planning. It's an important question to wrestle with as we all seek to be good stewards of our time and resources. If that's you, I invite you to turn the page and read about how one week can truly transform your church. If you are a skeptic and not sure how you even got this book, then I challenge you to look at VBS with fresh eyes and an open heart. Together, let's discover why VBS is truly worth it.

Jana Magruder
Director
LifeWay Kids

1 WE ARE IN CRISIS

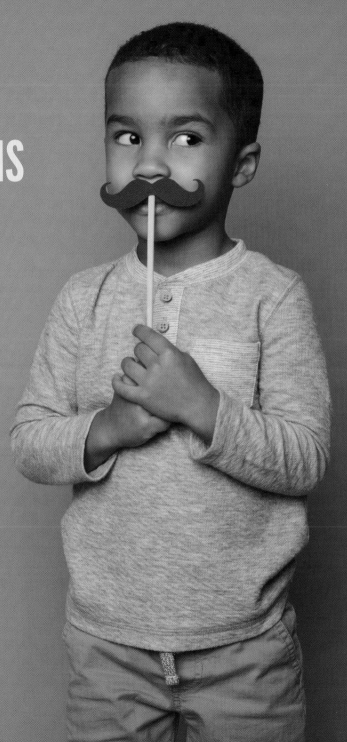

1 CHURCHES AND INDIVIDUALS ARE IN CRISIS

THE CHURCH IS IN CRISIS

JESUS CAME NEAR AND SAID TO THEM, "ALL AUTHORITY HAS BEEN GIVEN TO ME IN HEAVEN AND ON EARTH. GO, THEREFORE, AND MAKE DISCIPLES OF ALL NATIONS, BAPTIZING THEM IN THE NAME OF THE FATHER AND OF THE SON AND OF THE HOLY SPIRIT, TEACHING THEM TO OBSERVE EVERYTHING I HAVE COMMANDED YOU. AND REMEMBER, I AM WITH YOU ALWAYS, TO THE END OF THE AGE." MATTHEW 28:18-20

Jesus gave His parting words to the disciples in the form of The Great Commission. If you're like me,[JM] you memorized it when you were young. I not only memorized it, I sincerely wanted to tell others about Jesus! As Christians, we don't want to hide our faith or keep it as an exclusive promise only for us—we want to share the gospel. It's good news for us and good news for everyone. The command begins with the word "Go," an action verb. Jesus could have said, "pray about telling others" or "wait and see if someone asks about Me." But, no—He said, "Go tell the world."

Brothers and sisters, evangelism is at the core of our faith. We currently live in a free country and are allowed to talk about Jesus openly in most contexts. Nothing is stopping us from inviting others to our churches. We do not live in a place where we risk our livelihood or lives to share the gospel. Yet, research tells us we are not doing it. In a survey of nearly 3,000 protestant churchgoers, 80 percent say they believe they have a personal responsibility to share their faith. However, 61 percent say they have not shared how to become a Christian with anyone in the past six months. In fact, 48 percent say they have not invited anyone to church in the past six months.[2] Does this surprise you? Maybe it does since many of us are in ministry and feel like we are sharing the gospel regularly. But are we really only sharing the gospel at church? How are you doing outside the walls of your church? Are you sharing the gospel regularly with friends, neighbors, and others in your life? Do these statistics describe the people in your church? Is evangelism a priority? I ask because these questions should make us uncomfortable. Sharing Jesus with those who don't know Him is what we as Christians are called to do. There is not an opt-out button.

At the same time, we have to consider the fact that tens of thousands of reported salvations can be traced back to VBS annually.[3] That fact alone

80% OF THOSE ATTENDING CHURCH 1 OR MORE TIMES PER MONTH BELIEVE THEY HAVE A PERSONAL RESPONSIBILITY TO SHARE THEIR FAITH ... BUT ARE THEY DOING IT?

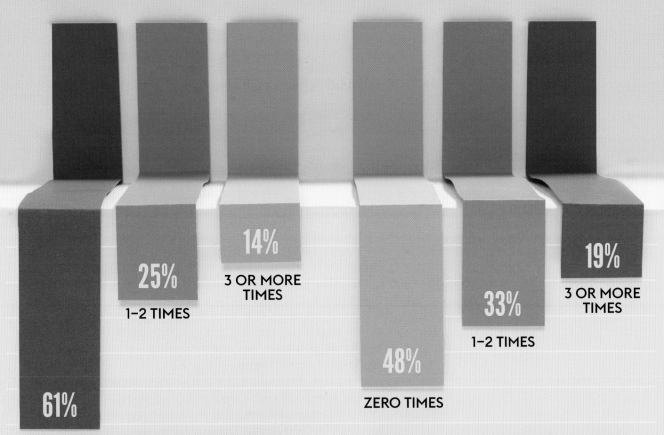

61%
ZERO TIMES

25%
1–2 TIMES

14%
3 OR MORE TIMES

48%
ZERO TIMES

33%
1–2 TIMES

19%
3 OR MORE TIMES

In the past six months, about how many times have I have shared how to become a Christian?

In the past six months, about how many times have I have invited an unchurched person to attend a church service or program?

is amazing and I could stop writing now if I felt like that number would hold. What's concerning is that fewer churches are doing VBS each year. A study by Barna Research states 81 percent of U.S. churches offered VBS in 1997. However, by 2012 only 68 percent of U.S. churches offered VBS.[4] The numbers are dropping. The Church has an evangelism crisis and one of the best methods of spreading the gospel is diminishing. It's time to face the problem head-on and realize that we have to approach this crisis with urgency.

INDIVIDUALS ARE IN CRISIS

In January of 2008, I became the proud owner of the first generation of the iPhone. I knew one friend who had one, but I didn't know much about what it did. To me, it was just an extension of the iPod—now there was a phone that could play your music! But, that wasn't the reason I wanted one. The reason I thought I needed one was because I completely missed a playdate for my daughter. We had spent Christmas with my in-laws and were still four hours away from home, having staying a couple of days into January until it was time to go home for school to start. I got a call on my Nokia phone from my friend back in Austin asking if my daughter and I were still coming to her house for the playdate. Well, honestly, I had not even thought of it. I totally forgot it was planned—my paper calendar was lost in luggage somewhere in the guest bedroom and I really wasn't paying attention to it anyway—I was on vacation. But, apparently, I had made big plans to make snowflake cookies on January 2 at my dear friend's house with our daughters. She was, of course, very understanding—no big deal—but I was mortified. I told my husband that day I wanted to buy an iPhone with my Christmas money. I remembered that this new smartphone had a calendar feature with reminders that would ding at you. I definitely needed that. Problem solved. Being a tech and gadget guru, he happily obliged my request and drove me to the AT&T store to get this new invention.

We got the phone all fixed up. For all four hours on the drive home (as a passenger), I marveled at setting up my calendar, reading all my emails—even the silly "forwards" my mom sent. I was hooked from the beginning,

THE CHURCH HAS AN EVANGELISM CRISIS AND ONE OF THE BEST METHODS OF SPREADING THE GOSPEL IS DIMINISHING.

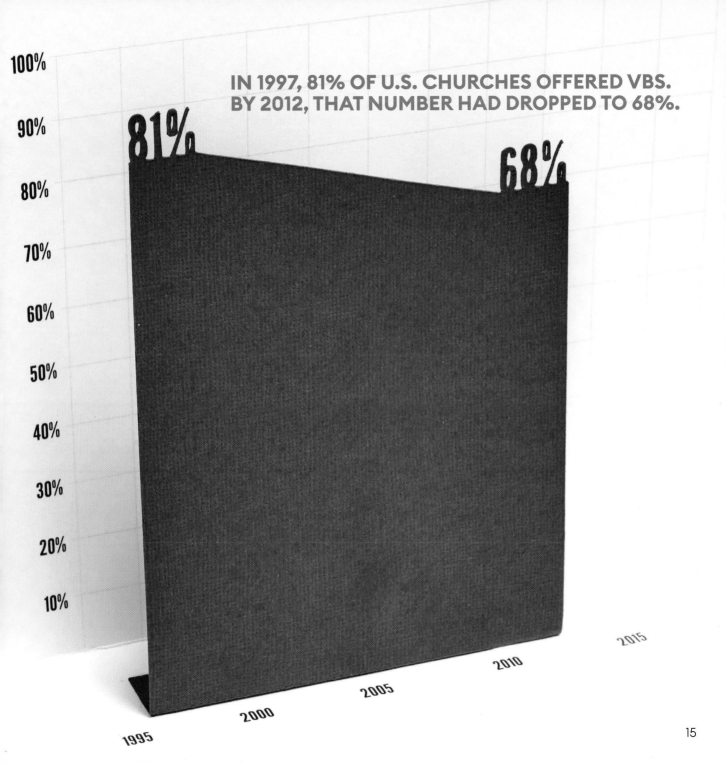

IN 1997, 81% OF U.S. CHURCHES OFFERED VBS. BY 2012, THAT NUMBER HAD DROPPED TO 68%.

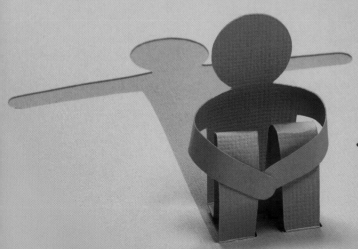

GENERATION Z REPORTS THE HIGHEST LEVELS OF
LONELINESS.

and that was before social media—yes, I was an early adopter of that, too. That phone changed my world and before I knew it, my friends, family members, everyone had a smartphone.

Most of us, if not all, own and think we *must have* our phones and tablets. We use them to conduct our personal and professional lives. We use them for business and pleasure. And somewhat innocently, many of us gave them to our kids in some format, a little too young.

Enter Gen Z—the generation you and I are ministering to each week. They are digital natives, never knowing the world without the Internet or smartphones. A Nielsen study in 2016 found close to half of kids (45 percent) who have a mobile phone and service plan, received it between the ages of 10 and 12.[5] Research also indicates many kids are reading actual books less. "In 2014, the number of 13-year-olds who said they rarely or never read for pleasure was 22 percent, a statistic that's almost tripled over the last three decades," writes Aaron Wilson.[6] So, what are they doing instead? They are on their phones, tablets, and gaming devices. They are photographing their food, their friends, themselves (hello selfies), and posting everything going on in their lives without actually living real-life experiences. Sure, they have friends—but are more concerned about followers and likes than true relationships. They text or snapchat more than they call on the phone or see each other in person. They watch Netflix or YouTube videos more than they participate in events and experiences with real people and social relationships.

Perhaps more concerning for all age groups is the fact that Americans are lonelier than they've ever been. In a new study, published by the global health service company Cigna, statistics show that 46 percent of U.S. adults report sometimes or always feeling lonely and 47 percent report feeling left out. These are considered to be "epidemic levels." Adults between the ages of 18 and 22, part of Gen Z were the loneliest generation, with a "loneliness score" of 48.3. Possible loneliness scores range from 20 to 80, with the national average a 44.[7]

ENTER GEN Z— THE GENERATION YOU AND I ARE MINISTERING TO EACH WEEK. THEY ARE DIGITAL NATIVES, NEVER KNOWING THE WORLD WITHOUT THE INTERNET OR SMARTPHONES.

Churches, individuals, and families are in crisis. We are addicted to our phones and we are lonelier than ever. But, what can we do about it? What is our role as the local church? These are fundamental questions that we as ministry leaders have to ask ourselves. In order to do that, we must look at our original mission and goals. The reason we do what we do is so that kids and teens will develop a relationship with Jesus and follow Him the rest of their lives.

If you consider the top 10 spiritual influencers in the life of a child or teenager, Bible reading emerges as the #1 thing we can do to help them grow up spiritually healthy.[8] This is a message for leaders in the church and parents and caregivers at home. Vacation Bible School places an emphasis on biblical literacy that can launch a lifetime in God's Word. Among Americans who attended VBS when they were growing up, 88 percent say "Participating in Vacation Bible School as a child helped me better understand the Bible."[9] It's called Vacation *Bible* School for a reason—a whole week dedicated to helping kids learn and grow in God's Word.

Research also tells us that kids and teens who have Christian friendships have healthier spiritual lives as adults. VBS can provide the opportunity to develop friendships through fun, real-life experiences. Similarly, kids and teens who connect with godly men and women at church have healthier spiritual lives into adulthood.[10] This message helps us cast a great vision as to why the whole church should pour into VBS. God did not create us to be lonely—He made us to live in community. There are very few times in the rhythm of church calendars that provide a whole week of human and multi-generational interaction for the sake of the kingdom of God. For that alone—VBS is worth it.

Yes, we are in a crisis. But, God has given us everything we need to work through it. When an entire local church wraps around a common goal of helping kids love the Bible, develop Christian friendships, and learn from godly men and women—we can have hope. In spite of a culture where smart device addiction and the loneliness epidemic seem to be winning, we can offer something better. We can invite others to our church and say, "Come in, sit by a new friend, open your Bible, and learn about Jesus from someone who loves Him." That, my friends, can transform your church.

THE HARVEST
IS ABUNDANT,
BUT THE WORKERS ARE FEW.

THEREFORE, PRAY
TO THE LORD OF THE HARVEST TO
SEND OUT
WORKERS INTO HIS HARVEST.
— MATTHEW 9:37-38

2 THE SOLUTION IS TIMELESS

The crisis that we as churches and individuals find ourselves in today is not new. People have always needed to hear God's redemptive plan. Even Jesus Himself declared, "The harvest is abundant, but the workers are few. Therefore, pray to the Lord of the harvest to send out workers into his harvest." (Matthew 9:37-38) The crisis of evangelism is rooted in history.

Neither is the reality of individual loneliness only a contemporary crisis. Adam was alone in the garden of Eden, Elijah felt isolated on Mount Horeb, and Jesus experienced ultimate loneliness when He cried out His last words on the cross. However, because of Jesus' horrific moment of complete and absolute loneliness, you and I do not have to be alone, ever. This is a message too good to keep to ourselves. We have hope to share with the world.

VBS began in a moment of crisis not so different from the one we face today—churches needed to spread the gospel, and individuals longed

> VBS BEGAN IN A MOMENT OF CRISIS NOT SO DIFFERENT FROM THE ONE WE FACE TODAY.

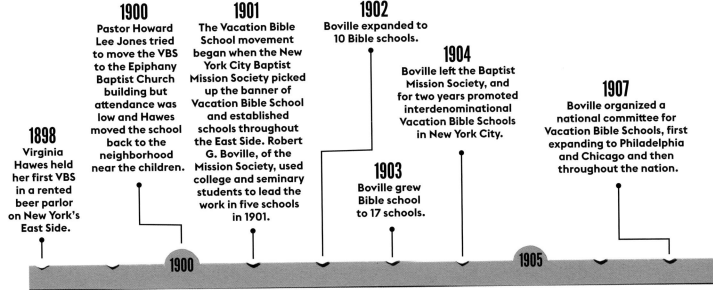

1898
Virginia Hawes held her first VBS in a rented beer parlor on New York's East Side.

1900
Pastor Howard Lee Jones tried to move the VBS to the Epiphany Baptist Church building but attendance was low and Hawes moved the school back to the neighborhood near the children.

1901
The Vacation Bible School movement began when the New York City Baptist Mission Society picked up the banner of Vacation Bible School and established schools throughout the East Side. Robert G. Boville, of the Mission Society, used college and seminary students to lead the work in five schools in 1901.

1902
Boville expanded to 10 Bible schools.

1903
Boville grew Bible school to 17 schools.

1904
Boville left the Baptist Mission Society, and for two years promoted interdenominational Vacation Bible Schools in New York City.

1907
Boville organized a national committee for Vacation Bible Schools, first expanding to Philadelphia and Chicago and then throughout the nation.

1900

1905

Virginia Hawes saw the misery of New York's East Side and chose to do something about it.

for meaningful community. Enter Virginia Hawes, a godly woman who noticed a problem and did something indicative of her go-getter personality—she began searching for a solution.

The year Virginia Hawes held her first Vacation Bible School, New York City's streets were a "clash of ugliness and beauty, comfort and inconvenience, elegance and grit." Filled with progress and promise, New York in 1898 had just merged into one city from many smaller towns and was known for wealth, decadence, and moral license. But some parts of town, crowded with immigrants hoping for a better life, were instead filled with poverty, disease, and "vast misery in the tenements and sweatshops."[11]

Hawes saw some of this misery in New York's East Side, just a mile from her church, the Baptist Church of the Epiphany. Hawes was the Virginia-born wife of a doctor, and was an active church member. People described her as having an intelligent mind, a warm heart, great faith, and as being a hard worker who was not easily fazed by obstacles.[12] This seems to have been just the right personality mix to kick off the VBS movement.

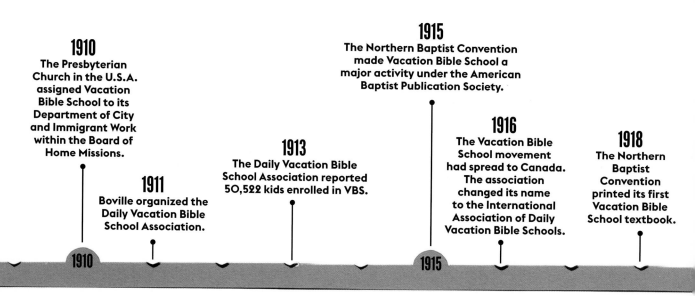

1910
The Presbyterian Church in the U.S.A. assigned Vacation Bible School to its Department of City and Immigrant Work within the Board of Home Missions.

1911
Boville organized the Daily Vacation Bible School Association.

1913
The Daily Vacation Bible School Association reported 50,522 kids enrolled in VBS.

1915
The Northern Baptist Convention made Vacation Bible School a major activity under the American Baptist Publication Society.

1916
The Vacation Bible School movement had spread to Canada. The association changed its name to the International Association of Daily Vacation Bible Schools.

1918
The Northern Baptist Convention printed its first Vacation Bible School textbook.

Hawes' son fondly remembered her role as a Sunday School teacher and her skills as a storyteller and advocate for children. "After class, the children used to hover around her, and if anyone spoke of illness in the family, she would almost invariably visit the home," he wrote. This was a class of 60–80 children, ages six through twelve, crowded in Epiphany's prayer meeting room.[13]

Hawes wrote and spoke with passion of the needs of the people in the East Side, urging listeners to give time and money to reach people "almost at our door" who needed the gospel, rather than only focusing on international efforts. While talking about the general needs of the people in her city, it's not hard to see the seeds behind VBS in her words.[14]

In 1897, Hawes raised enough money to keep the church doors open when the trustees had decided to close it down, knowing the people in the area needed the church. Then in 1898 she turned her energy to another project to help her community—VBS.

In 1897, Hawes raised enough money to keep the church doors open.

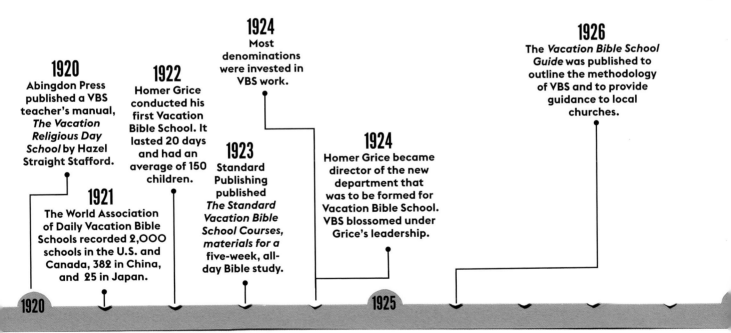

1920
Abingdon Press published a VBS teacher's manual, *The Vacation Religious Day School* by Hazel Straight Stafford.

1921
The World Association of Daily Vacation Bible Schools recorded 2,000 schools in the U.S. and Canada, 382 in China, and 25 in Japan.

1922
Homer Grice conducted his first Vacation Bible School. It lasted 20 days and had an average of 150 children.

1923
Standard Publishing published *The Standard Vacation Bible School Courses*, materials for a five-week, all-day Bible study.

1924
Most denominations were invested in VBS work.

1924
Homer Grice became director of the new department that was to be formed for Vacation Bible School. VBS blossomed under Grice's leadership.

1926
The *Vacation Bible School Guide* was published to outline the methodology of VBS and to provide guidance to local churches.

1920
1925

A 1916 article about her life explained, "Mrs. Hawes observed that after the public schools closed the streets and open squares in a near section of the East Side swarmed with idle and sometimes unruly children." Hawes decided something needed to be done.[15] While such conditions were clearly unsafe, Hawes was more concerned about the damage to children's character by being unoccupied and uneducated about the Bible and the gospel.

"We felt that the Bible is not taught in homes as it used to be, nor as it should be, and it is not taught in the public schools. So we opened ... a school in which we made the Bible our only text book," Hawes said.[16] Though other summer schools of this kind seem to have taken place as far back as the 1870s, Hawes' school is looked on as the foundation for VBS in its modern form.[17]

For this first VBS, "no attraction was offered but Bible stories and great kindness."[18] Bible stories and great kindness were enough, however. Records don't exist for 1898, but in 1899, Hawes and others kept detailed records of the second Daily Vacation Bible School, as it was called. On the first day, 114 children attended.[19]

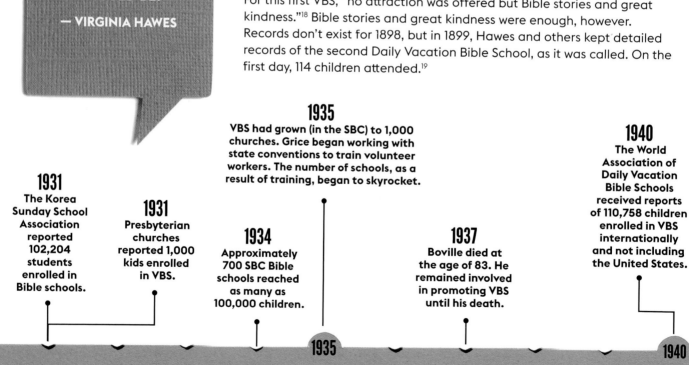

1931
The Korea Sunday School Association reported 102,204 students enrolled in Bible schools.

1931
Presbyterian churches reported 1,000 kids enrolled in VBS.

1934
Approximately 700 SBC Bible schools reached as many as 100,000 children.

1935
VBS had grown (in the SBC) to 1,000 churches. Grice began working with state conventions to train volunteer workers. The number of schools, as a result of training, began to skyrocket.

1937
Boville died at the age of 83. He remained involved in promoting VBS until his death.

1940
The World Association of Daily Vacation Bible Schools received reports of 110,758 children enrolled in VBS internationally and not including the United States.

1935

1940

IT'S WORTH IT

Both years, Hawes found a convenient space to rent: a beer parlor, unused during the day and close to the children attending the school. Apparently undisturbed by the building's usual purpose, she rented several rooms and began. In 1900, Epiphany's pastor tried to move the school to the church, but attendance dropped dramatically because of the distance children had to come, and the school was moved to another building near the beer parlor.[20]

Hawes paid her teachers in those early years of VBS. She usually had three classes, one for older boys, one for older girls, and one for a mixed group of younger boys and girls.[21] Children sang hymns, memorized long passages of Scripture, made crafts, and studied the Bible together.

"They often surprised us by questions about Scriptures that showed that they not only committed to memory the Word of God, but that they understood and reasoned about it," Hawes wrote of the pupils in 1900.[22]

"A great many questions were asked about living the Christian life, which (was) explained to mean loving God and trying to do His will, and could only be entered upon by being born again," wrote Annie Burns, teacher for the older girls, in a report on that summer. "Quite a number of them said they thought of God only with a feeling of terror, and all agreed that that feeling must be changed before they could enter the kingdom of heaven, and so they could see the necessity of the new birth."[23]

From the early days of VBS, the gospel has been foundational and available to people of all nationalities. Many of Hawes' students were among New York's vast immigrant population. Dr. Robert Boville continued the evangelistic tradition of VBS, effectively launching a VBS "movement" in 1901. Most likely having heard of Hawes' work through

The beer parlor Hawes rented for VBS, along with the $25.00 receipt for its rental.

1951
Many denominations celebrated the fiftieth anniversary of the VBS movement. Experts commemorated the date with information about the history of VBS and its continuing importance.

1945

1950

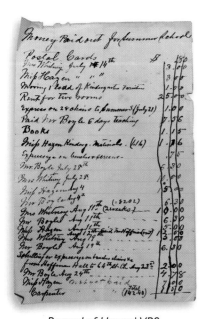

Record of Hawes' VBS expenses, including teachers' salaries and the beer parlor rental.

1953

Homer Grice retired from his work at the Sunday School Board. His associate since 1938, Sibley C. Burnett, took over editing VBS materials and promoting VBS work.

connections they had, Boville started five different vacation Bible schools.[24]

Almost from its inception, VBS has been a global movement. Over his years of VBS work, Boville extended the movement first nationally, and then internationally.[25] Ralph Mould, director of Children's Work for the Presbyterian Church in the U.S.A., would say in 1951, "Psychological barriers of being economically, socially, racially, or nationally 'across the tracks' have a way of collapsing before the advance of a vacation school. This means that the vacation school is probably one of the most widening experiences in Christian fellowship the average church ever provides for its children."[26]

By 1916, VBS was "accepted as one of the established, most blessed means of sowing gospel seed in places where otherwise it might never fall."[27] Especially because of its length—Hawes' first schools lasted six weeks—many practitioners realized they had an extended chance to impact children's lives.

At first the vacation schools were interdenominational, but gradually different church denominations began to pick up the program and make it a part of denomination-wide work until, by 1924, most denominations were invested in VBS work.[28]

In 1922 another intense personality picked up the banner of VBS. Homer Grice was a young pastor in Georgia and was struck by the growing VBS trend. His church, First Baptist Church of Washington, GA, built a new education building in 1920. Grice and his wife Ethel wanted to see the space used. So they decided to embark on a VBS journey of their own, holding their first school in the summer of 1922.[29]

1955

1960

In 1924, LifeWay, then known as the Baptist Sunday School Board, made Grice a job offer. Up until this time, Southern Baptists as a denomination hadn't been doing VBS, and the publishing company wanted to help change that. Grice began producing LifeWay's first VBS curriculum in an empty office, with only a desk and a chair.

Grice hired writers, taught them what he thought the curriculum should be, and then edited their work into a cohesive set in time for the summer of 1925. He said the Holy Spirit had inspired him with a vision for VBS reaching multitudes and he felt that to do that, curriculum must be usable by the most inexperienced teacher. Grice also spent extensive time traveling the country, educating churches about the benefits and best practices of VBS.

Those writing about Grice portrayed him as larger than life. He was described as a "physical and mental giant," a man of "tremendous energy," enthusiasm, with a genius for leadership and organization. By 1951, when churches were celebrating the 50th anniversary of VBS as a movement, Grice's denomination alone recorded 1.9 million students and 300,000 faculty.

"Few men are given the privilege of leading in their lifetime a mighty army of Christian men and women to spend their energies in blessing and teaching child life," wrote Sibley Burnett, a coworker of Grice's,

Homer Grice's signature stamp

1970
The first Vacation Bible School Institute was conducted to introduce the new materials. It was so successful that it launched a new strategy for training local associations and state conventions, which then replicated the trainings for churches.

1970
The standard pink, blue, yellow, red, and green spiral-bound cycle and group-graded curriculum books were replaced with an all-new annually dated curriculum. Along with the new curriculum came a new age-grading basis and new terminologies.

1965   1970

> **"THE VACATION SCHOOL IS PROBABLY ONE OF THE MOST WIDENING EXPERIENCES IN CHRISTIAN FELLOWSHIP THE AVERAGE CHURCH EVER PROVIDES FOR ITS CHILDREN."**
> — RALPH MOULD

in 1951. Ethel Grice worked enthusiastically alongside her husband, writing about and promoting VBS.[30] Though the Grices never had children, they parented millions of children through VBS.[31]

Many recognized, in the years leading up to Grice's retirement, the contribution he made to VBS. "His whole personality was placed into the movement and has been spent for its advancement," wrote Jerome Williams, secretary of education and promotion for the Baptist Sunday School Board. "He has thought, prayed, planned, read, dreamed, written, talked, preached, and promoted Vacation Bible School work. There is power in a consecrated personality."[32]

VBS survived some difficult years. In 1916, the first large epidemic of polio hit New York, and it was probably this epidemic that impacted attendance that summer.[33] A 1917 report from the International Association of Daily Vacation Bible Schools showed that attendance dropped by about 12,000 because of an epidemic in 1916. Still, the association reported that 60,812 children attended VBS in the summer of 1916.[34] The epidemic did not stop VBS.

War also cast its shadow over VBS, but even World War II could not stop the progress of this powerful ministry. In 1942, Grice wrote that children "have never needed the Vacation Bible School as much as they need it now," and urged churches not to stop this important ministry, providing suggestions for how to pull this off under war conditions, with fewer helpers and supplies running scarce.[35]

The World Association of Daily Vacation Bible Schools published reports from VBS around the world in 1940, including moving notes from France

1980   1985

and Germany. VBS workers in France gathered 200 children in the southern mountains, many of whom had to continue fleeing the war and many of whom were separated from their parents. A card from Germany read, "Christ is powerful among you and whether He is crucified in our weakness yet He lives in God's strength, and if we are also weak in Him, yet we live with Him in God's strength."[36]

Neither disease nor war could deter God's work through VBS. Historically, churches have felt the impact of VBS deeply. It has been known to help plant a new church or revive a dying one. God also has used VBS to raise up new church leaders. "It is gratifying to see ... that many of our top church leaders today got the 'feel' of leadership through the Vacation Bible school. They responded to instruction, gained confidence, grew rapidly, and developed nobly into our best leadership," said Dr. James Sullivan, a pastor in Abilene, Texas, in a 1953 article on VBS.[37] Sullivan would go on to become the president of the Baptist Sunday School Board.

In addition, "Some of the best Sunday School teachers I know today are those who were discovered in Vacation Bible school," said Andrew Allen, State Sunday School Secretary for Texas in 1953. "Many college and seminary young people have found such delight in working in the schools they have volunteered their services for other religious activities."[38]

The leaders Sullivan and Allen reference—as well as leaders like you and I[BB]—are indebted to VBS pioneers such as Virginia Hawes and Homer Grice. The work of these two consecrated personalities echoes worldwide today, wherever VBS is taught. Grice himself always pointed back to the

1997
LifeWay (then the Baptist Sunday School Board) introduced a brand new format for Vacation Bible School. This new format included a theme; rotation sites for music, missions, crafts, recreation, and snacks; a renewed evangelistic emphasis; custom music written specifically for the theme; video with daily drama segments; and even a VBS musical.

1990
Themes were introduced into VBS materials. However, these were not the kind of immersive themes we know today.

1992
Southern Baptist Vacation Bible School hit an enrollment record of 3,709,174.

1996
Group Publishing published its first VBS material.

1990

1995

> "I LOVE TO LIVE AMONG THE CHILDREN, TO LABOR TO THE BEST OF MY POOR ABILITY FOR THEM."
> — VIRGINIA HAWES

hard work and perseverance of Virginia Sinclair Hawes and her legacy of unselfish work. This became a work carried on by countless Christians across the world, willing to give up time from their summers to help children come to know Jesus.

"This Summer School was undertaken for the good of children," Hawes wrote. "I love to live among the children, to labor to the best of my poor ability for them, and to find my last resting place among them would be sweet peace."[39] And indeed the resting place of her legacy is among the children of VBS who hear, every year, of the love of Christ and the power of the gospel because of her pioneering work.

Virginia Sinclair Hawes, Homer Grice, and godly persons like them discovered a timeless solution to the age-old crisis of evangelism and individual loneliness—Vacation Bible School. The research cited in this book validates the timeliness of this solution.

2005
LifeWay introduced two VBS Preview events in Nashville and Glorieta, New Mexico. VBS leaders from across the country had the opportunity to explore VBS resources, experience a VBS worship rally, and preview the VBS musical performed by a local children's choir.

2008
Special Friends curriculum was created to provide resources for those teaching children, teens, and adults with special needs.

2003
Spanish translations of the preschool and children's resources were introduced.

2000

 2005

I[LH] truly believe that God desires to continue to use VBS as a tool of the church to reach families with the gospel. And, I'm convinced that the solution to loneliness is found in the message of Jesus taught in VBS.

Dr. Sullivan also saw VBS as an effective way to reach whole families for Christ. "If there is a single infallible entree into any home in the community it is through the child. Gain the confidence of the child and you win the friendship of the parents."[40]

VBS is worth it—all the effort, all the expense, all the hours, all the tears. Why? Because VBS is the one week that mobilizes the entire church to reach the community with the gospel, while simultaneously providing a unique discipleship experience for the individual child and volunteer.

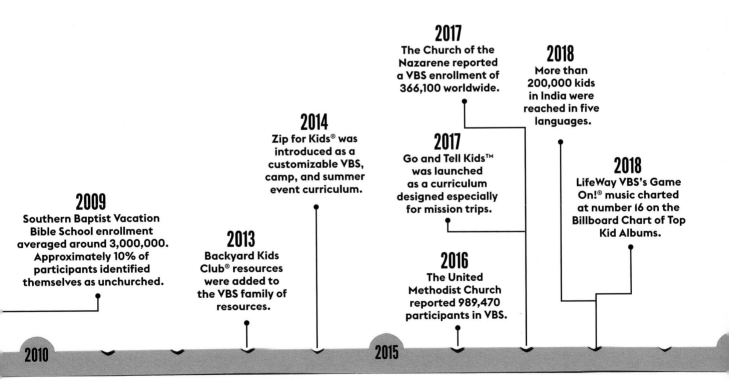

2017
The Church of the Nazarene reported a VBS enrollment of 366,100 worldwide.

2018
More than 200,000 kids in India were reached in five languages.

2014
Zip for Kids® was introduced as a customizable VBS, camp, and summer event curriculum.

2017
Go and Tell Kids™ was launched as a curriculum designed especially for mission trips.

2018
LifeWay VBS's Game On!® music charted at number 16 on the Billboard Chart of Top Kid Albums.

2009
Southern Baptist Vacation Bible School enrollment averaged around 3,000,000. Approximately 10% of participants identified themselves as unchurched.

2013
Backyard Kids Club® resources were added to the VBS family of resources.

2016
The United Methodist Church reported 989,470 participants in VBS.

2010

2015

2 IT'S WORTH IT ...
BECAUSE THE
GOSPEL IS GLOBAL

1 IT'S WORTH IT ...
BECAUSE VBS IS ABOUT JESUS

GO! DISCIPLE! REMEMBER!

Go!—The Great Commission—most of us have read it, memorized it, and gotten the prize from the treasure box at church. As soon as someone mentions it, we kick into auto repeat and rattle it off in the translation popular at the time we were learning it. But, for many people, its meaning is as forgotten as the plastic toy from the treasure box. Can we pause a moment and look with fresh eyes at this powerful mandate by our Savior and Lord?

As mentioned in the first chapter of this book, "Go," is an action verb. In fact the Greek word translated as "go" is a form of the verb that indicates continuing action—"while you are going," or "having gone."[1] Whether you are going about your daily business or intentionally going beyond your home base to share the gospel, the bottom line is that we have the biblical mandate to go with the gospel.

VBS remains one of the primary ways the local church champions the cause of "going." The debate is not really "what's more effective, opening the church doors and compelling them to come in versus packing up and moving out into the community?" But rather, "while you are going" and whatever you are doing, be involved—intentional action that shares the gospel and helps disciple believers.

Based on annual church reports, more than 65,000 salvations are reported as having been a result of VBS annually.[2] When the numbers of VBS were up, so were the reported professions of faith and, sadly, when the numbers of VBS were down, reported professions of faith were less. It's not so much that VBS was the key to successfully sharing the gospel, but rather, it appears churches did nothing to take the place of

GO, THEREFORE, AND MAKE DISCIPLES OF ALL NATIONS, BAPTIZING THEM IN THE NAME OF THE FATHER AND OF THE SON AND OF THE HOLY SPIRIT, TEACHING THEM TO OBSERVE EVERYTHING I HAVE COMMANDED YOU. AND REMEMBER, I AM WITH YOU ALWAYS, TO THE END OF THE AGE.

–MATTHEW 28:19-20

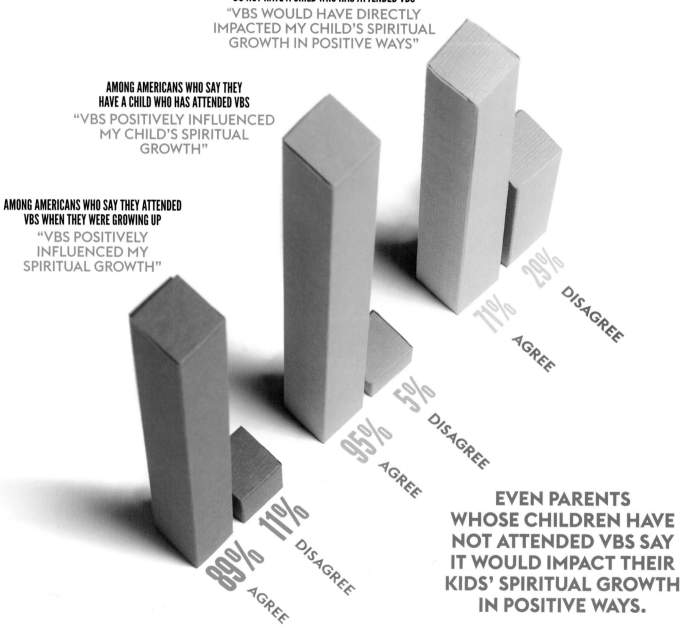

AMONG AMERICANS WHO SAY THEY ATTENDED
VBS WHEN THEY WERE GROWING UP

"VBS POSITIVELY
INFLUENCED MY
SPIRITUAL GROWTH"

AMONG AMERICANS WHO SAY THEY
HAVE A CHILD WHO HAS ATTENDED VBS

"VBS POSITIVELY INFLUENCED
MY CHILD'S SPIRITUAL
GROWTH"

AMONG AMERICAN PARENTS WHO SAY THEY
DO NOT HAVE A CHILD WHO HAS ATTENDED VBS

"VBS WOULD HAVE DIRECTLY
IMPACTED MY CHILD'S SPIRITUAL
GROWTH IN POSITIVE WAYS"

89% AGREE   11% DISAGREE

95% AGREE   5% DISAGREE

71% AGREE   29% DISAGREE

**EVEN PARENTS
WHOSE CHILDREN HAVE
NOT ATTENDED VBS SAY
IT WOULD IMPACT THEIR
KIDS' SPIRITUAL GROWTH
IN POSITIVE WAYS.**

this concentrated evangelistic effort when they dropped VBS from their ministries.

Besides the local church effort, VBS has also been a key go-to option for community outreach plans that focus on kids such as backyard kids clubs or neighborhood VBS programs. VBS is often the format used by local church mission groups that travel across their state or around the world to share the gospel. Almost weekly the LifeWay VBS team is blessed with pictures and stories of kids in other countries who gather to sing the songs, make the crafts, and most importantly hear the Bible stories and the invitation to trust Jesus as Savior. Often the stories include parents or other adults—standing along the sidelines watching and listening—who also came to a saving knowledge of Jesus. The footprint of VBS truly GOES, and goes into all the world.

Disciple!—Out of all of the verbs in the Great Commission, this one has prominence in the Greek grammatical style. It is the word that should be said with the most direction and force. In fact, it takes the Greek noun for "disciple" (mathētēs) and uses it in the verb form (matheteuō). So, basically it's like saying in English, "Disciple!"[3] While you are going (an important part of the mandate) and while you are baptizing those who profess their faith in Jesus, and while you are teaching—make disciples.

The church incorporates many tools in her mission of making disciples— small group Bible studies, one-on-one mentoring, community groups, and in today's world, even social media groups. Nevertheless, VBS continues to be one of the foremost local church endeavors that provides opportunities to begin and continue the work of engaging people with the gospel, and "teaching them" as part of the disciple-making process.

Sometimes the enemy intimidates us by making us think the general public is resistant to anything church related. However, LifeWay Research revealed some interesting statistics. First, among Americans who said they attended VBS when they were growing up, 89 percent agree that VBS positively influenced their spiritual growth. And, it doesn't stop there. Among Americans who say they have a child who has attended

THE FOOTPRINT OF VBS TRULY GOES, AND GOES INTO ALL THE WORLD.

VBS, 95 percent agree that participating in VBS positively influenced their child's spiritual growth. But, what is most amazing to me[RV] is that among American parents whose kids did not attend VBS, 71 percent agree that participating in VBS would have directly impacted their child's spiritual growth in positive ways.[4]

Overwhelmingly, people who have experience with VBS and those who haven't share the same perception: VBS can impact the spiritual growth of a child in a positive way. VBS provides the dual purpose of introducing participants to Jesus Christ and providing valuable spiritual growth opportunities for those precious—and sometimes precarious—early steps of discipleship.

When you recognize the fact that our research shows that about twice as many kids attend a church's VBS as their weekly ongoing programming for kids, it maximizes the opportunity to impact the spiritual growth of more kids than ever.[5]

Remember!—The Great Commission would be truly daunting if it stopped with "Go!" and "Disciple!" But, thanks be to God, Jesus sealed this command with a promise. "Remember, I am with you always, to the end of the age." Any effort to expand the kingdom of heaven is of no value unless it is empowered by God's Spirit. However, as we pour ourselves into going, baptizing, and telling in order to make disciples, we have the promise of God's presence and power. We are not alone.

The driving message of VBS is the same whether you have five kids or five thousand, whether you are in a megachurch or on a mission trip, whether you have high-tech production resources or simply your Bible and a teaching picture. The driving message is the gospel of Jesus Christ. And the driving purpose is found in the words of Jesus: Go! Disciple! Remember, I am with you!

> "VBS IS A LOCAL MISSION TRIP THAT JUST ABOUT ANY CHURCH CAN DO."
> — SAM RAINER

2 IT'S WORTH IT ...
BECAUSE VBS ATTRACTS

VBS is synonymous with summer in many church settings. Why? Perhaps because, as we've already discovered, VBS has been around in one form or another since at least 1898, when Virginia Hawes hosted street kids in a New York City beer parlor. Under the current moniker, VBS has been a local church and denominational evangelistic strategy since the 1920s. And to me,[MT] one of the best signs of VBS's health and stability is its longevity. In kids ministry, which is sometimes marked by trendy, short-lived fads, VBS is one of the few ministries with real staying power.

Rather than being a sign of its irrelevance, I would argue that VBS's historical longevity proves it is a dependable ministry and a successful strategy. In fact, in the last reporting, Southern Baptists had almost 2.5 million enrolled in VBS, the United Methodist church had 989,470, and the Church of the Nazarene 366,100. If we could see all of the churches in other denominations and non-denominational churches we would see even more millions of people every summer attracted to VBS.[6] Talk about impact!

"OK, but surely there are other summer events I could do that could have that same kind of impact? Why does it have to be VBS?" I'll let you in on a little secret. VBS has a level of brand awareness that even a Fortune 500 company would covet. Let's take a look at some of the stats.

- 6 out of 10 American adults have attended VBS at some point in their lives. (Is there anything that nearly two-thirds of the entire American adult population have ALL done except maybe drink water?)
- Of those who attended VBS, 9 out of 10 have positive memories of VBS and 81 percent even said it was a highlight of childhood!
- 61 percent of those who never even attended a VBS have a positive view of it.[7]

VBS HAS A LEVEL OF BRAND AWARENESS THAT EVEN A FORTUNE 500 COMPANY WOULD COVET.

ADULTS WHO ATTENDED VBS HAVE OVERWHELMINGLY POSITIVE MEMORIES OF THE EXPERIENCE.

6 OUT OF 10
AMERICAN ADULTS HAVE ATTENDED VBS

9 OUT OF 10
HAVE POSITIVE MEMORIES OF VBS

8 OUT OF 10
SAID IT WAS A CHILDHOOD HIGHLIGHT

Looking at these numbers, an overwhelming negative perception of VBS simply doesn't exist. Perhaps a small segment of the population has some wariness when it comes to VBS, but not many. VBS is something the vast majority of adults experienced as children, and it's something they remember fondly. It's is something parents want their kids to experience, too. Even people who never attended VBS themselves view it in a positive light. VBS is not something they want their kids to stay away from.

Here's another staggering statistic. More than two-thirds of American parents (69 percent) say they would encourage their child to attend VBS at a church they don't attend if their child was personally invited by a friend. Let that sink in a moment. That's 69 percent of ALL American parents—not just Christian or "churched" parents. That includes Muslim parents, Buddhist parents, agnostic parents—parents from every socioeconomic status.[8]

Why would we walk away from this kind of brand awareness? We don't have to explain what VBS is or try to convince people of the benefits. All we have to do is say, "Come with me!" Now let me be clear—a real invitation is more than just posting a link to the church website or social media page. It's more than leaving flyers around the neighborhood. Something as important as introducing people to the gospel requires a personal invitation. So if we feel like VBS isn't working or is no longer attracting new kids and their families, we must ask ourselves,"Have we stopped inviting?"

Everyone can issue a personal invitation—older adults can invite neighborhood kids, and kids themselves can invite their friends. I am amazed every summer that the number of kids who show up at my church's VBS is at least twice what we run on Sunday mornings! VBS is something parents are looking for. In fact, sometimes, parents send their kids to multiple Vacation Bible Schools throughout summer. Whatever the reason VBS attracts kids and parents, own it! Celebrate it! Capitalize on it! Do it up right!

"But VBS is so expensive! To do something that kids want to attend and want to bring their friends to is going to blow my entire annual budget in just one week!" Here's a word of wisdom from Forbes: "It's worth noting that brands do better in tough times compared to unbranded products."[9]

MORE THAN TWO-THIRDS OF AMERICAN PARENTS (69%) SAY THEY WOULD ENCOURAGE THEIR CHILD TO ATTEND VBS AT A CHURCH THEY DON'T ATTEND IF THEIR CHILD WAS PERSONALLY INVITED BY A FRIEND.

SOMETHING AS IMPORTANT AS INTRODUCING PEOPLE TO THE GOSPEL REQUIRES A PERSONAL INVITATION.

62% OF NON-CHRISTIAN OR UNCHURCHED AMERICAN PARENTS STATED THAT THEY ARE AWARE OF AT LEAST ONE CHURCH NEAR THEM DOING VBS.

IF WE FEEL LIKE VBS ISN'T WORKING OR IS NO LONGER ATTRACTING NEW KIDS AND THEIR FAMILIES, WE MUST ASK OURSELVES, "HAVE WE STOPPED INVITING?"

VBS is a brand that nearly everyone knows. In fact when surveyed, 62 percent of non-Christian or unchurched American parents stated that they are aware of at least one church near them doing VBS.[10] So if I am only able to do one big thing all year to reach my community with the gospel, I'm going with the one thing that is most recognizable! The "brand name" event is my best shot for attracting my community. Therefore, VBS is a worthwhile and lasting investment.

In addition, VBS doesn't have to be a budget-buster to be successful. Here are a few ideas to keep in mind:

- Make wise choices when it comes to curriculum and decorations.
- Choose a curriculum that includes a variety of activities so that it is possible to pick and choose those that best match your budget and resources.
- Look for a curriculum that provides quality music, video, and multimedia resources. (This is often the easiest way to make VBS feel fresh and relevant to an unchurched audience.)
- Look for a curriculum that provides teachers with everything they need (posters, templates, etc.), so that they don't have to waste time or money looking for or creating the extra things they need.
- Allow church members to donate supplies or purchase specific resources from a list.
- Share decorations with other churches.
- Keep the energy level high. Kids will match the level of excitement and enthusiasm modeled for them. It's what allows them to have a good time and create lasting memories. Best of all, enthusiasm is free!

Remember, Vacation Bible School has been carefully stewarded for over a century as an effective tool for sharing the gospel. The reason VBS remains attractional and so important is because it gives churches the opportunity to impact lives for eternity as kids, teens, and adults come to know the saving power of Jesus Christ. That alone makes VBS worth it!

"We want the next generation to know our great God. We also want to draw families in—many families will come to church because their children want to come to church. We believe you can combine fun, energetic environments and activities that make children want to come and be super intentional about using all things to teach and weave the truths of Scripture into their lives while they are here."
— VBS LEADER

3 IT'S WORTH IT ...
BECAUSE VBS ENERGIZES

Walking into a church the day before VBS begins elicits one of the most exhilarating feelings you could ever experience. Whether it is the stage team building and assembling the set in the worship center, the teachers gathering all of the craft supplies and Bible study teaching materials, or the VBS director racing around making sure that everything is just right—the environment and atmosphere are electric. The enthusiasm building for the week of VBS is palpable.

We know VBS attracts people from the community, but what is it about VBS that gets an army of church members out of their seats and hot-gluing googly eyes or leading wacky games? What is it that propels churches all over the country and across the globe to use VBS, bringing new life to their ministries? Churches have a strong desire to teach the gospel to every kid who walks through their doors, shows up at a park, or sits on the grass in a backyard, but why do they choose VBS?

Let's be honest. VBS is fun! What other time of the year does your kids minister agree to be plastered in the face by a pie? VBS innately can unite a church in a way that few other ministry events can. A couple of years ago during VBS I[1k] witnessed some of the most joyful worship I had ever experienced. That year one particular VBS song described the joy that we have when Jesus is in our lives. Many of the leaders took this message to heart. As they performed the hand motions in unison and moved to the music, I became aware that these moments mean so much more than just bright colors and catchy tunes. The leaders were worshiping God, and their joy could not be kept to themselves—it was contagious!

When that energy is contagious it begins to spill out of our church doors and into the community. In fact, there are stories of churches that "caught fire" after introducing VBS into their summer programming. A church plant in a small Pennsylvania town was experiencing difficulty in

VBS LEADERS SPEAK...

"WE WORK TOGETHER AND WE WORK HARD! AGAIN, ALL WORKING TOWARDS THE SAME GOAL."

"THE MOST MEANINGFUL EXPERIENCES ARE THOSE WHEN I GET TO WATCH SOMEONE STEP INTO A ROLE THAT THEY DIDN'T THINK THEY COULD DO WELL, AND THEY REALIZE THEIR POTENTIAL AND GROW SO MUCH THROUGHOUT THE WEEK."

"A POSITIVE ASPECT OF VBS FOR OUR CHURCH IS THAT IT SENDS EVERYONE INTO THE REST OF SUMMER RE-ENERGIZED ABOUT OUR MINISTRY."

"THE MOST MEANINGFUL MOMENTS OF VBS ARE SEEING CHILDREN EMBRACE FAITH IN JESUS CHRIST ... AND OUR ADULTS BECOME PASSIONATE ABOUT ENGAGING KIDS WITH THE GOSPEL."

"VBS IS MY FAVORITE TIME OF YEAR ON THE MINISTRY CALENDAR."

"SO FOR ME, I WANT TO MAKE SURE VBS IS A FUN ENVIRONMENT KIDS WANT TO COME AND BE A PART OF."

VBS CREATES ENERGY IN THE LOCAL CHURCH BECAUSE AT THE CENTER OF ALL THE FUN AND CRAZINESS IS THE TRUTH OF GOD'S WORD.

establishing a solid membership base. The church, started by six people, seemed to be on the brink of fizzling out. One member decided she was going to help host a VBS for the neighborhood children. Soon families were bringing their kids and learning more about the church. The church grew to serve 55 families.[11]

The energizing effect of VBS is not limited to kids or to current church leaders. Many kids ministers use VBS as a tool to recruit new volunteers. In fact, 64 percent of churches use VBS as a way to create excitement for their kids ministry.[12]

I had the privilege to work with a new leader this summer who, other than being a parent herself, had never taught a small group Bible study. I knew she was apprehensive when she walked in the door on day three, notes in hand. However, this novice teacher told the story of Thomas seeing Jesus alive in a way that captivated the kids. With her background in law, she was able to share this eye-witness account and connect it to each child's thoughts and feelings. The kids immediately understood the message of the Bible story. The next day this same new leader came in with new energy and confidence.

VBS creates energy in the local church because at the center of all the fun and craziness is the truth of God's Word. That truth should permeate your entire church. In fact, whenever a group of believers strives toward the single focus of uplifting the gospel, amazing things happen. The result is immense joy and excitement, and volunteers discover VBS is worth the effort required to prepare and reach their community with the gospel of Jesus Christ.

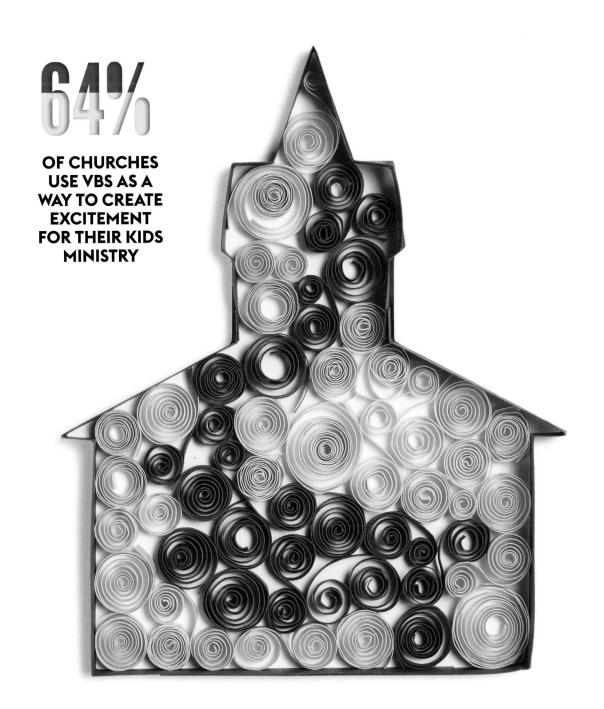

64%

OF CHURCHES USE VBS AS A WAY TO CREATE EXCITEMENT FOR THEIR KIDS MINISTRY

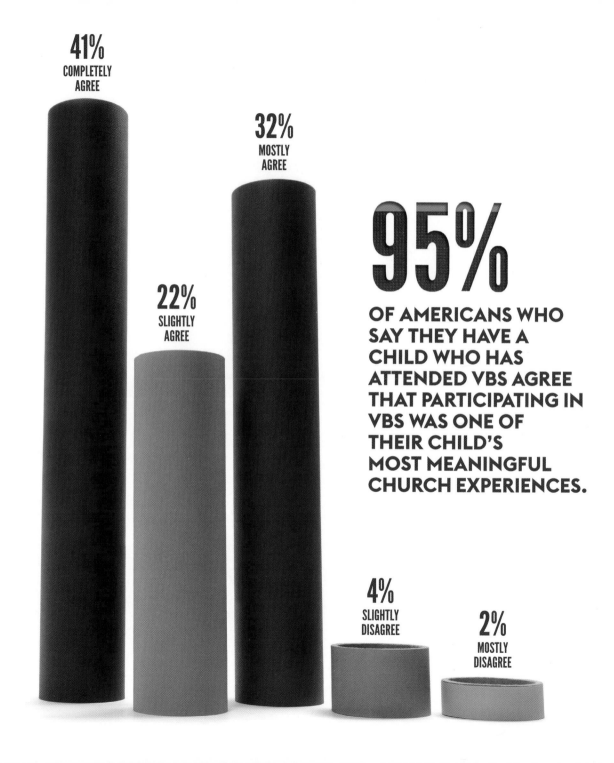

41%
COMPLETELY AGREE

32%
MOSTLY AGREE

22%
SLIGHTLY AGREE

4%
SLIGHTLY DISAGREE

2%
MOSTLY DISAGREE

95%

OF AMERICANS WHO SAY THEY HAVE A CHILD WHO HAS ATTENDED VBS AGREE THAT PARTICIPATING IN VBS WAS ONE OF THEIR CHILD'S MOST MEANINGFUL CHURCH EXPERIENCES.

4 IT'S WORTH IT ... BECAUSE VBS MOBILIZES TO REACH

Not only does VBS energize the church, VBS mobilizes the local church to reach its community with the gospel. When reading the research about VBS, I[GB] was strongly reminded of the movie *Field of Dreams*, when character Ray Kinsella hears a voice whisper to him, "If you build it, he will come." Churches are notorious for "building" events and expecting people to just show up. That's not quite enough. As we've said earlier, the research shows that if you personally invite people, they will come.

So, how do we mobilize our churches to reach our communities? As part of our research into VBS practices, we listened to church leaders tell us about their experiences. One leader said, "VBS is an opportunity where many types of people can get involved—whether in the preparations, donating resources, or working with children during the week of the event."[13] What that tells us is that teenagers, college students, single adults, newlyweds, married adults with and without kids, empty nesters, and senior adults all come together with one singular goal—to help create a life-transforming, gospel-centered VBS experience for every single boy and girl. As one respondent so aptly stated, "This is a church event, not just a children's ministry event."[14]

What drives this volunteer army of myriad ages, gifts, and talents to pour so much of themselves into one week of VBS? Why do they invest so much of their time and energy? Instead of vacationing in the mountains or at the beach, why do they use their vacation days—sometimes all their vacation days—to teach and lead at VBS? Ask any member of this vast VBS army and you'll find their answer is quite simple. There is no better investment of time and God-given talent than sharing the gospel of Jesus Christ with kids. That's it. VBS provides the opportunity to speak faith, hope, love, and truth into kids' lives instead of the false hope, conditional love, and half truths they are bombarded with each and every day. Perhaps that's why 95 percent of Americans whose child has attended VBS agree that it was one of their child's most meaningful church experiences.

To see this diverse group of people roll up their sleeves and work together to share Christ with kids is to see the body of Christ in action. As one kids ministry leader put it, "People who normally do not work with children, work with children. Afterwards, they loved it so much, they want to continue in the fall! Hardly any other event bridges the gap between generations."[15] What a privilege to be a part of such a tremendous team—warts and all! Or maybe I should say, "Just as I am, including all my faults."

I'm quite certain my "warts and all" often cause me to feel intimidated when participating in church outreach and evangelism. What I've discovered, however, is that VBS provides an excellent way—and even a fun way—to overcome that feeling of intimidation. It's so easy to tell a parent what we talked about in VBS on any given day, and parents are eager to hear what their children learned. In the short span of a week, these brief "Jesus conversations" with parents can grow into relationships with eternal impact. My feelings of inadequacy and fear of what to say are quickly overcome.

Like so many others who volunteer to serve during VBS, I've realized God's "power is perfected in weakness," in my warts and in my all. (2 Corinthians 12:9) Echoing my feelings of inadequacy, another church leader confesses, "It is God who is working in me, and I continually need Him to sustain and direct me ... You don't have to have a huge giftedness for teaching children in order to be a contributing member of our VBS team. We serve together, side by side. So if you don't have the answer, someone beside you does! For our church, it's an opportunity to come together and experience community throughout the week. And that, in itself, is so valuable!"[16] Personally I'm grateful God chooses to use me, warts and all, for His glory.

Such was the case for Mr. Jim, whose kids ministry leader shared this story: "One year we had a little guy who went under the table in the fellowship hall. Crying and all that stuff. Mr. Jim sat with him under the table all

69% OF AMERICAN PARENTS WILL ENCOURAGE THEIR CHILD TO PARTICIPATE IN A VBS EVENT AT A CHURCH THEY DON'T ATTEND IF INVITED BY ONE OF THEIR FRIENDS.

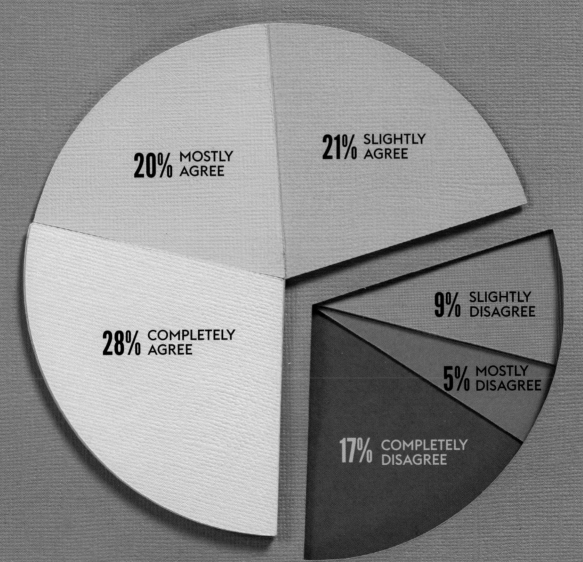

20% MOSTLY AGREE

21% SLIGHTLY AGREE

28% COMPLETELY AGREE

9% SLIGHTLY DISAGREE

5% MOSTLY DISAGREE

17% COMPLETELY DISAGREE

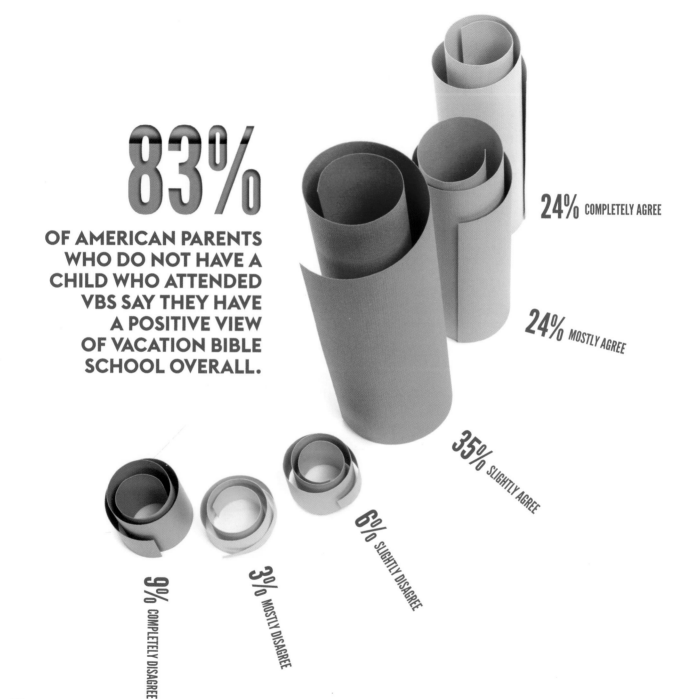

83%

OF AMERICAN PARENTS WHO DO NOT HAVE A CHILD WHO ATTENDED VBS SAY THEY HAVE A POSITIVE VIEW OF VACATION BIBLE SCHOOL OVERALL.

24% COMPLETELY AGREE

24% MOSTLY AGREE

35% SLIGHTLY AGREE

6% SLIGHTLY DISAGREE

3% MOSTLY DISAGREE

9% COMPLETELY DISAGREE

evening! They did the Bible story, made a craft, talked, and ate. All under the table! The next night the little boy was so excited to arrive and he rotated with his class ... and Mr. Jim!"[17] God chose to use Mr. Jim for His glory, and that little guy under the table had a great week. So did Mr. Jim!

Like Mr. Jim, the lives of VBS leaders are often transformed by the gospel, not just the lives of kids who attend. "We work together and we work hard! Again, all working towards the same goal," stated one such leader. "It's the only time in our ministry that we spend the week together serving and bonding. It's like an at home missions trip. When the week is over, we're all exhausted, kids included. But we can see God's hand in the week and celebrate together how He worked in people's lives. Sometimes that work is in the children's lives and other times it's in the lives of a volunteer. Either way, it's powerful to all experience together."[18] As rewarding and empowering as it is to work together as the body of Christ with a clear and common goal, I've also learned it's not about me. It's about the kids. If we invite them, they will come!

Since reaching kids with the gospel of Jesus Christ—kids in our churches and in our communities—is our motivation, we must do all we can to get them to come. Building strong, Christ-centered foundations of faith, hope, love, and truth in our kids is of the utmost importance. As one VBS leader reminds us, the most meaningful moments of VBS are "seeing kids take steps at the end of the week to grow their relationship with Jesus."[19]

Meaningful church experiences can and do happen for kids during the week of VBS. Even among parents whose child has never attended VBS, 83 percent say they have a positive view of Vacation Bible School overall.[20] That means, then, that the likelihood of parents accepting an invitation for their kids to attend VBS is extremely high. In turn, those same kids go home and tell their parents. Working with kids at VBS opens doors of opportunity to invite their parents to church. "I also take great pleasure in meeting new families from our community who are moving or maybe have never come to an evangelistic church before," admits a church leader. "I love introducing them to our church family, our

"IT'S THE ONLY TIME IN OUR MINISTRY THAT WE SPEND THE WEEK TOGETHER SERVING AND BONDING. IT'S LIKE AN AT HOME MISSIONS TRIP."
—VBS LEADER

programming, and answering questions for them. VBS truly is a great outreach tool in our community!"[21]

Another leader told us in our research that, "The most meaningful moments of VBS are seeing children embrace faith in Jesus Christ, seeing our students become leaders, and seeing our adults become passionate about engaging kids with the gospel. VBS is a total church experience unlike any other. All five of our generations serving alongside each other: senior adults, median adults, young adults, students, and children."[22] In order for VBS to be a true mobilizer of the church, we must accept the responsibility that VBS is a *total* church endeavor.

In doing so we realize that there is no better investment of time and God-given talent than sharing the gospel of Jesus Christ with kids, teenagers, and adults. VBS is worth the investment. Regardless of our own weaknesses, faults, inabilities, and shortcomings, God will strengthen us for the task. He always does. All we need to do is obey Jesus' command to make disciples. Invite them. They will come.

"Every year we have people who take their ONLY vacation to volunteer at VBS."

–VBS LEADER

5 IT'S WORTH IT ... BECAUSE VBS MOBILIZES TO TEACH

GOD GIVES EACH GENERATION, EACH LEADER, EACH INDIVIDUAL BELIEVER UNIQUE QUALITIES AND GIFTS. ALONE, EACH ONE HAS MERIT, BUT WHEN EVERYONE BRINGS HIS OR HER GIFTS TO THE TABLE, FAR GREATER IMPACT IS MADE THAN ANY ONE INDIVIDUAL CAN DO ON HIS OWN.

From the youngest child to the oldest adult, and from the senior pastor to the newest member, Vacation Bible School is a time the entire church body can come together united to spread the gospel. Each generation brings its own perspective to the teaching experience, enhancing the learning experience and expanding the reach of the message. With revivals being a thing of the past for many churches, VBS is often the most intentional week on the church calendar.

This week should be a priority of the entire church, starting with the senior pastor. In every worthwhile endeavor of the church, the senior pastor is ultimately responsible for leading an intergenerational army of church staff and volunteers in the church's mission to go and make disciples. And, VBS is no exception to Paul's reminder that Jesus calls church leaders to equip "the saints for the work of ministry, to build up the body of Christ." (Ephesians 4:12)

In fact, through the Holy Spirit, God gives each generation, each leader, each individual believer unique qualities and gifts. Alone, each one has merit, but when everyone brings his or her gifts to the table, far greater impact is made than any one individual can do on his own.

For example, below is a list of qualities generally attributed to specific generations:

SILENT (1928–1945)	BABY BOOMERS (1946–1964)	GENERATION X (1965–1979)	MILLENNIAL (1980–1995)	GENERATION Z (1996–2014)
Loyal	Productive	Entrepreneurial	Technological	Independent
Disciplined	Mentors	Individualistic	Scheduled	Most racially diverse generation
Risk averse	Traditionalists	Questions authority	Assertive[23]	Competitive[24]

**WHEN ALL GENERATIONS COME TOGETHER,
EACH OFFERING UNIQUE SKILLS AND GIFTS,
AN IMAGE OF THE GOSPEL BEGINS TO EMERGE.**

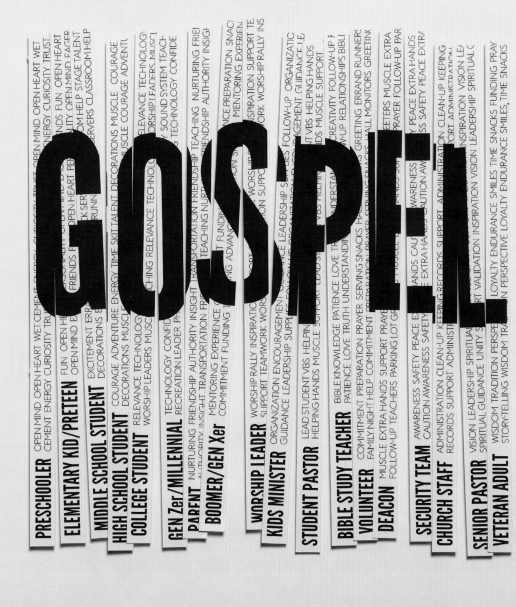

IT'S WORTH IT

"Seeing adults engaging with the next generation for the sake of the gospel is always a meaningful experience."
— VBS LEADER

When people from each generation serve side-by-side you get the best team possible. While it may seem that a Gen Xer who questions authority might not be a good team member, keep in mind that she can help your church stay relevant. Still, it's good to have those loyalists and traditionalists on board to remember why you do some of the things you've always done.

VBS offers one of *the* best teaching and galvanizing tools available. This comes to light as you witness:

- an awkward teen being mentored by a Boomer teacher—how he now steps up to the plate and leads a small group;
- the eye-opening experience a veteran teacher has as she learns new technology tips from a Millennial;
- a senior adult greeting parents and kids at the door and see the smile on his face as he realizes he still has value;
- a deacon helping a preschool mom in from the parking lot;
- a senior pastor engaging in worship rally alongside the kids in the pews.

When we can get past thinking that the only participants in VBS are the teachers and the kids, we'll realize that indeed it is a whole church event. From the prayer team to the security team to those who gather and donate supplies, everyone can find a place to fit in. Each role pours into the lives of kids. Iron sharpening iron. Generation teaching generation. The body of Christ working together, sharing the gospel. And, it's worth it!

9 OUT OF 10 ADULTS WHO ATTENDED VBS GROWING UP AGREE THAT VBS BOTH POSITIVELY IMPACTED THEIR SPIRITUAL GROWTH AND HELPED THEM BETTER UNDERSTAND THE BIBLE.

VBS IS A NATURAL TRAINING GROUND FOR DISCIPLING LEADERS.

6 IT'S WORTH IT ... BECAUSE VBS MOBILIZES TO LEAD

Just as God equips the church to mobilize for teaching the gospel, God also issues the call to bring others alongside us. That's called discipleship. Discipleship is woven into the very fabric of VBS. First there's the expected layer of discipleship as children, teens, and adults study the Bible and are challenged to grow in their relationship with Jesus. That's one of the main reasons we do VBS. It's also one of the expected outcomes. Nearly 9 out of 10 adults who attended VBS growing up agree that VBS both positively impacted their spiritual growth and helped them better understand the Bible.[25] However, there are other layers of discipleship occurring naturally in VBS that may not be as obvious.

As new leaders work alongside seasoned veterans, they too are being discipled. As teenagers learn the ropes of service from adult mentors, discipleship is taking place. This layered discipleship model is not present in all church programming. But in VBS, it's common practice. That is one of the beauties of VBS—it's a natural training ground for discipling leaders.

VBS is an easy "first serve" opportunity for young and new leaders. It's a short-term commitment that allows people to serve in ways that are comfortable or appealing to them personally. Whether that is in a classroom, in the sound booth, on security detail, or in the kitchen assembling snacks—there's a place for everyone to serve! However, volunteers need a few things in order to feel successful in their roles:

- Clearly communicated expectations
- Simple job descriptions
- Training
- Mentoring
- Partnering with experienced leaders
- Excellent, flexible curriculum materials

"I love the layers of discipleship that exist in VBS. Obviously, children are discipled. But I pair seasoned leaders with new teachers and witness leadership developed. We have volunteers from every age and life stage that interact with one another. ... This is a church event, not just a Children's Ministry event."
–VBS LEADER

When a volunteer feels successful about his experience serving in VBS, he is more likely to return again next year. Entire teams may have enjoyed teaching together so much that they sign up to work together again year after year. VBS can be a great time to strengthen relationships within the church!

For new church members, serving in VBS may be just the thing needed to help them feel connected. Through VBS they can make new friends, learn the church campus, and get to know other families. Parents may gain a new level of trust as they become familiar with policies and procedures while serving, or develop a new respect for the people who teach their children week after week. It's not uncommon to hear things like, "I had no idea kids could learn so much!" or "Who knew teaching 4-year-olds was so much fun?"

It also is not uncommon for a volunteer to sign up to help for "just one week of VBS" and feel God's tug on her heart to work with kids every week. In fact, it was after teaching VBS in a park in New Mexico that I[MT] first heard God calling me to serve Him by teaching preschoolers. Mine is not a unique testimony. God consistently uses VBS to raise up individuals as teachers to disciple younger generations toward becoming Christ followers.

I'll let you in on a little secret: those of us who teach children every week know there is an extra special layer of discipleship taking place in that sacred space. Not because of what we are imparting to children, but in what we are learning *because* we teach children. The personal study that goes into preparing to teach, the unique ways in which children view the world, and the insightful questions they ask constantly challenges, convicts, and encourages me personally. Corrie Ten Boom was right when she observed, "The best learning I had came from teaching."[26]

The value of training in developing and discipling volunteer leaders cannot be overstated. Resist the urge to just "put warm bodies in the room" in order to survive the week of VBS. Take the time to intentionally prepare, train, and equip volunteers to lead successfully. The good news

> "THE BEST LEARNING I HAD CAME FROM TEACHING."
> — CORRIE TEN BOOM

is most people don't mind coming to a VBS training session. It's usually fun and fast-paced. Everyone is excited to get a glimpse of the theme, hear a bit of the music, sample a themed snack, and gather some ideas for decorating. So, capitalize on their interest and use the time to intentionally develop volunteers as leaders.

As you train leaders, help them develop realistic expectations. Guide them to understand the characteristics and abilities of the ages they will teach. Provide practical strategies for guiding behavior, and allow seasoned teachers to share what has worked well for them. Walk through the curriculum materials, and teach volunteers how to use them. For new volunteers, simply handing them a leader guide and then walking away may leave them feeling overwhelmed. So teach them what to look for, how to pick and choose activities, and how to adapt the curriculum to match their schedule, supplies, and particular group of kids. Empower volunteers to lead by giving them permission to make the curriculum their own. Most importantly, share expectations for the week, and cast a vision so that each volunteer may see how his or her role helps accomplish the purpose of your church's VBS.

VBS is unique in that every aspect is intentionally designed to provide opportunities for evangelism. Every activity, every rotation, every song is especially crafted to fit the main biblical point of the day, making it possible for every person the child encounters throughout their VBS day to "live out" the gospel in front of them. That makes the job of every VBS volunteer—every VBS leader—important! Snack ladies are no longer "just snack ladies." Recreation leaders are not just responsible for wearing kids out so that they can sit still and listen longer during Bible study. Each point of engagement becomes an opportunity to talk to a child about what the Bible teaches and about what the Holy Spirit might be saying to him or her.

The number one thing we can do for VBS leaders is to help them view their responsibilities through the lens of the gospel. This allows them to approach their role with renewed purpose. Everything they say or do is teaching something about who God is. Every conversation they

THE NUMBER ONE THING WE CAN DO FOR VBS LEADERS IS TO HELP THEM VIEW THEIR RESPONSIBILITIES THROUGH THE LENS OF THE GOSPEL.

33%

OF CHRISTIAN, CHURCH-ATTENDING PARENTS SAY THEY WANT LEARNING FROM TEACHERS AND VOLUNTEERS TO HAVE THE BIGGEST IMPACT ON THEIR CHILD DURING A VBS EVENT.

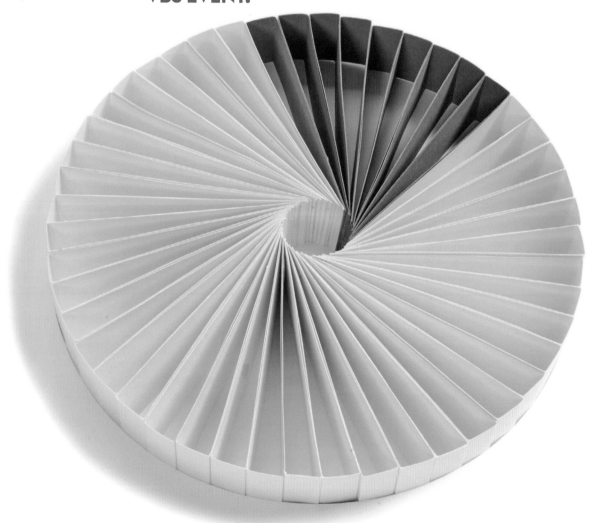

have with a child can be used to build a relationship of trust and love that may afford them the opportunity to later share the gospel. In one denomination, salvation decisions consistently average about 1.1 times the number of leaders who are trained.[27] Why? Because trained leaders are intentional leaders.

Trained leaders understand their role and purpose in VBS. They believe their work is important. They understand that their primary responsibility during VBS is to point people to Christ. They harness the tools of VBS (crafts, songs, games, Bible stories, activities, etc.) effectively to help them share the gospel. Trained leaders are sensitive to the Holy Spirit and how He may be working in the life of a child. Their eyes are fixed on the goal of sharing the good news. They know it's worth it, because each child's eternity is worth it.

FOR EVERY ONE VBS LEADER WHO IS TRAINED, THERE ARE 1.1 SALVATION DECISIONS.

7 IT'S WORTH IT ... BECAUSE VBS RELATES TO PARENTS

"ULTIMATELY WE CARE THAT THE CHILDREN AND FAMILIES HAVE THE OPPORTUNITY TO KNOW THE LOVE OF CHRIST AND SALVATION."

Up to this point, we have focused primarily on the individuals present during their respective VBS events—kids, leaders, teachers. And there's a reason for that. Through the years, most churches have focused mainly on kids in VBS. The goal was to get as many as we could in the doors of the church. And of course, to share the gospel with each and every one of them. Not bad goals. But VBS holds a hidden gem—the opportunity to build relationships with parents and families of these kids.

As one children's minister said, "These are opportunities for us as a church family to build connections to our community and neighbors, to help them see that we care about helping their children have great experiences and learn new things, but that ultimately we care that the children and families have the opportunity to know the love of Christ and salvation—even if they don't know that they need that."[28]

Today's parents have so much more to worry about than they did even five years ago. They feel they have less and less control over their kids' lives, inside and outside of the home. Threats are everywhere—unmonitored social media, violent video games, bullying, drugs, suicide, peer pressure, sex trafficking—the list goes on and on. We as a church can offer support in unique ways that a secular program can't. But first, we have to build trust. We have to build relationships.

One avenue for that is VBS. As we consistently show parents that we love their kids, that their kids are safe, that we're here to help—not judge—eventually we will earn their trust. As a result of that trust, we often are afforded opportunities to share the gospel with kids and their parents.

The good news is that overall, the majority of parents agree that attending VBS was a positive experience for their child. In fact, 95 percent of Americans whose child has attended VBS agree that participating in VBS was a positive experience for their child. And, as we have already

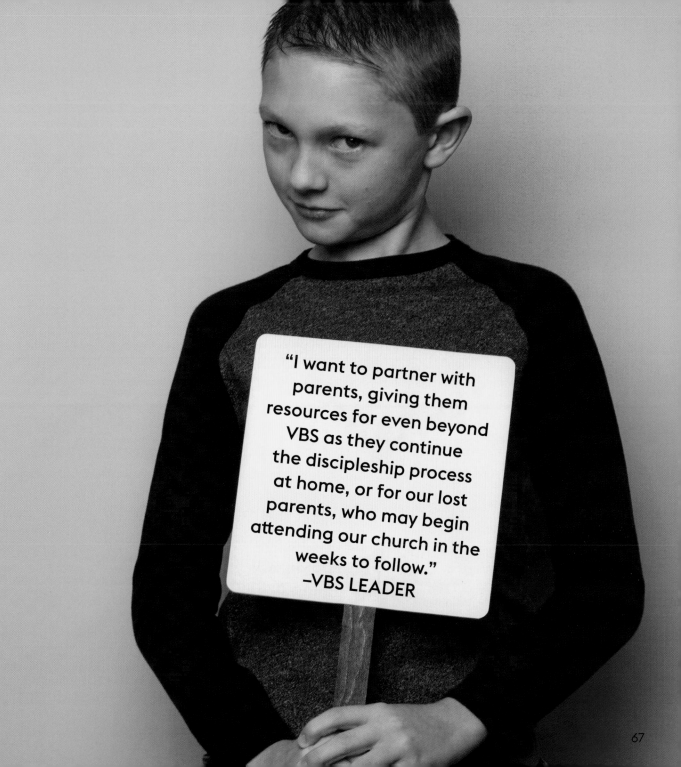

"I want to partner with parents, giving them resources for even beyond VBS as they continue the discipleship process at home, or for our lost parents, who may begin attending our church in the weeks to follow."
–VBS LEADER

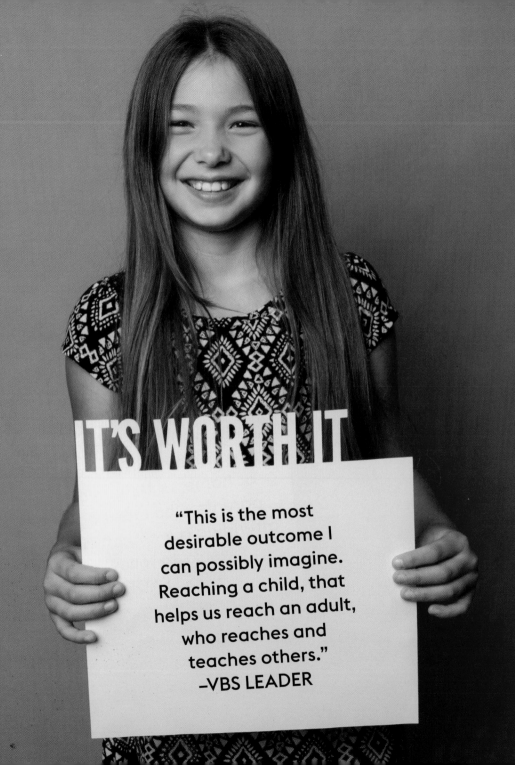

IT'S WORTH IT

"This is the most
desirable outcome I
can possibly imagine.
Reaching a child, that
helps us reach an adult,
who reaches and
teaches others."
–VBS LEADER

seen, 83 percent of parents whose kids didn't attend still have a positive view of VBS.[29] So why would we not do it?

Irrespective of this data, we continue to hear from churches that don't see a need to offer VBS because they have the impression their communities are saturated with it. However, more than half—53 percent to be exact—of parents with kids under the age of 19 reported that their kids have never attended.[30] That's more than 5 kids out of 10 who are not being reached by VBS! Imagine the possibilities of reaching 50 percent more kids and parents than you did last year! What glory to God that would be!

Still, others sometimes are tempted to complain that families are just using VBS as inexpensive childcare. And, the problem is? Even if more than 10 percent of your kids are attending your VBS for this reason, who cares? They're hearing the gospel. You're helping a parent. You're building a bridge. One VBS leader told us, "This is the most desirable outcome I can possibly imagine. Reaching a child, that helps us reach an adult, who reaches and teaches others."[31]

Some churches not only assure parents that their children are well cared-for during VBS, they also find other ways to engage parents—both inside and outside their church. Just a few examples are discipleship groups, marriage classes, and parenting seminars. These activities, along with traditional family night experiences, are designed to strengthen families and disciple parents. VBS helps build that bridge to reach them.

So, is it worth it? If you reach even one kid, one parent, one family—it's worth it.

95 PERCENT OF AMERICANS WHO SAY THEY HAVE A CHILD WHO HAS ATTENDED VBS AGREE THAT PARTICIPATING IN VBS WAS A POSITIVE EXPERIENCE FOR THEIR CHILD.

8 IT'S WORTH IT ... BECAUSE VBS WORKS

When I[BB] was growing up, my dad was the pastor of a small church in North Carolina. The church threw impressive energy into VBS every year, and I have fond memories of astronaut food and giant ocean-themed stuffed animals. Every year, I helped my incredibly creative mom turn the sanctuary stage into a boat, spaceship, or campsite.

But my favorite part was the yearly musical. Kids choir members started working on it as soon as the Christmas musical was done each year. We'd wait anxiously while our director decided on parts, then we'd spend the entire spring semester memorizing lines and learning songs. Kids visiting just for VBS joined the choir. In this way, half the year was invested in VBS-related activities, not just for our VBS director, but for much of the church.

Ours was not the only church to put so much time and effort into VBS. Our research shows that 78 percent of churches that host a VBS use it as their largest outreach to unchurched kids.

With 64 percent of churches that have a VBS event relying on VBS to create excitement about their children's ministries and the same amount using VBS to disciple kids within the church, churches are investing enormous time and effort each year, the way my church did when I was growing up.[32] In light of this, the most important question to ask is, does VBS work? Does it follow through on its promises? Does this ministry successfully spread the gospel? Yes, according to the research, we can confidently say, VBS works!

Each year, LifeWay collects data from churches doing VBS regardless of the curriculum publisher. While many churches do not report their results, LifeWay annually learns of more than 65,000 new commitments to Jesus Christ connected to VBS.[33] This means that a project that is taking up a lot

> DOES VBS WORK? DOES IT FOLLOW THROUGH ON ITS PROMISES? DOES THIS MINISTRY SUCCESSFULLY SPREAD THE GOSPEL?

CHURCHES USE VBS AS THEIR LARGEST OUTREACH TO UNCHURCHED KIDS.

78% USE VBS AS THEIR LARGEST OUTREACH TO UNCHURCHED KIDS IN A GIVEN YEAR

64% OF CHURCHES RELY ON VBS TO CREATE EXCITEMENT ABOUT THEIR CHILDREN'S MINISTRIES

64% USE VBS TO DISCIPLE KIDS WITHIN THE CHURCH

2,494,059
PEOPLE ENROLLED
IN VBS

21,376
CHURCHES REPORTED
A VBS

$7,012,010
GIVEN TO MISSIONS
DURING VBS

160,926
PROSPECTS DISCOVERED
THROUGH VBS

65,301
SALVATION DECISIONS
FROM VBS

835
DECISIONS MADE FOR
VOCATIONAL MINISTRY
AT VBS

YEAR AFTER YEAR, THE TIDE OF VBS NUMBERS REFLECTS INDIVIDUAL LIVES CHANGED FOR ETERNITY

*2017 SBC

of time and financial resources in church life is giving enormous returns in reaching people with the gospel, and discipling them in their faith.

"I count it one of the most effective agencies we have in the promotion of everything from evangelism to the teaching of the 'all things' commanded by the Saviour," wrote J. Howard Williams of the Baptist General Convention of Texas in 1951, on the 50th anniversary of VBS. "I still count the Vacation Bible School as the most immediately practical way of increasing the Bible study time of our children and youth," added J.L. Corzine, Sunday School Secretary for South Carolina.[34]

"Wait, that was almost 70 years ago! What does that have to do with my church today?" you may be asking. Additional statistics prove that VBS still works as a viable evangelistic tool of the local church. In 2017 among SBC congregations, there were almost 2.5 million people enrolled in VBS and 65,301 professions of faith reported.[35] Since not every church reports its numbers each year, there were very likely more salvations that year as a direct result of VBS.

As one kids ministry leader said, "VBS is unique in that it provides a concentrated dose of biblical teaching to our own children, as well as the opportunity to reach the lost in our community with the gospel of Christ. As someone who has a heart for reaching children, VBS is like the Super Bowl of children's ministry events." Another leader summed up the main point of VBS, "It all goes back to the gospel for me."[36]

Not only are children being reached with the gospel, often they're hearing it during the summer—a time when they are typically away from school and other responsibilities—and can concentrate on the heart-transformative message they're hearing and experiencing at VBS. Kids also have more hours of Bible study in that one week than in months of normal church attendance.

As churches debate whether VBS is worth their time and investment, it's time to ask, what else could replace this valuable vehicle for the gospel in children's lives? Churches report significantly smaller involvement in other

"VBS IS LIKE THE SUPER BOWL OF CHILDREN'S MINISTRY EVENTS."

summer activities for kids, even ones with spiritual depth like camp and mission trips, than they have in VBS.[37] If churches stop doing VBS, how will millions hear the gospel and tens of thousands make new commitments to Jesus Christ?

"We will have over 600 folks on our campus all week long learning and serving. We have not been able to repeat that in any other area of ministry. Even our 'large' one-time, all-in church experiences (fall festival, etc.) never have the intergenerational support or connection that VBS provides," explained one leader. "I love seeing all generations together at one place engaged in one purpose."[38]

If we stop doing VBS, we'll lose other benefits, too. While sharing the gospel and discipling kids are the main purposes for VBS, there are other beneficial outcomes, as well. VBS is a vital way to recruit and inspire kids leaders, helping them learn and grow in new ways.

One kids leader explained, "A positive aspect of VBS for our church is that it sends everyone into the rest of summer re-energized about our ministry. We find VBS a great tool for recruiting fall teachers and helpers. After a long school year all my teachers and helpers are tired and sometimes a bit burned out. The combination of a break in their teaching schedule for the summer and the excitement of VBS gives them what they need to want to come back and commit for another season."[39]

All this proves what I knew in my heart the first time I tasted dehydrated astronaut ice cream. We have invested our time, energy, and finances in the right thing. VBS is worth all this investment because VBS works.

"We will have over 600 folks on our campus all week long learning and serving. We have not been able to repeat that in any other area of ministry."
–VBS LEADER

3

IT'S WORTH IT ...
BECAUSE THE GOSPEL IS PERSONAL

1 IT'S WORTH IT ... BECAUSE VBS CONNECTS KIDS WITH JESUS

In the previous chapter, we established that more than 65,000 reported salvations are directly related to VBS each year.[1] It is natural to ask, "What about churches that don't report? Would that change the number?" Mathematically that's hard to discern. But, testimonies from churches around the world attest to the spiritual impact VBS has on their churches and communities. In fact, according to our research, when asked "How does VBS fit into your church's overall ministry?" 78 percent responded that it was used as their largest outreach to unchurched kids. When you combine that with the 64 percent who said they use VBS to disciple kids within their church, it becomes abundantly clear that VBS connects kids with Jesus on many levels.[2] Kids are introduced to who Jesus is and encouraged to develop a growing relationship with Him.

We know that VBS works, but why? The answer partially lies in the fact that a concentrated time of learning for consistent days with leaders committed to the job generates results. This can be said of any type of learning from sports camps to band camps to computer camps. However, when you include the power of God's Holy Spirit to equip teachers and speak to young hearts, the answer is evident. VBS works because of the concentrated energy, effort, prayer, and focus on the gospel inherent in VBS.

Vacation Bible School is unique because local churches have used it to reach an ever-changing generation of kids with the unchanging gospel. VBS has touched generations from "The Greatest Generation" (those born before 1928) through our current group of school-age kids (Gen Z).[3] However, unlike former generations, the current group of kids are often the children of adults who have little or no connection to a local church. Many have no acquaintance with the gospel. That's why most intentional VBS resources provide a very foundational approach to biblical truth. The good news is that research also tells us Gen Z is open to faith-based

> UNLIKE FORMER GENERATIONS, OUR CURRENT GROUP OF KIDS ARE OFTEN THE CHILDREN OF ADULTS WHO HAVE LITTLE OR NO CONNECTION TO A LOCAL CHURCH. MANY HAVE NO ACQUAINTANCE WITH THE GOSPEL.

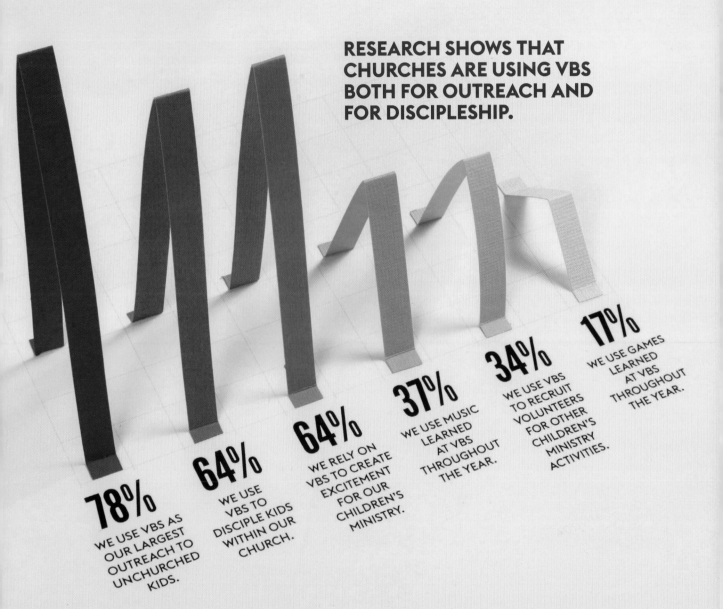

RESEARCH SHOWS THAT CHURCHES ARE USING VBS BOTH FOR OUTREACH AND FOR DISCIPLESHIP.

78%
WE USE VBS AS OUR LARGEST OUTREACH TO UNCHURCHED KIDS.

64%
WE USE VBS TO DISCIPLE KIDS WITHIN OUR CHURCH.

64%
WE RELY ON VBS TO CREATE EXCITEMENT FOR OUR CHILDREN'S MINISTRY.

37%
WE USE MUSIC LEARNED AT VBS THROUGHOUT THE YEAR.

34%
WE USE VBS TO RECRUIT VOLUNTEERS FOR OTHER CHILDREN'S MINISTRY ACTIVITIES.

17%
WE USE GAMES LEARNED AT VBS THROUGHOUT THE YEAR.

VBS REACHES EVER-CHANGING GENERATIONS WITH THE UNCHANGING GOSPEL.

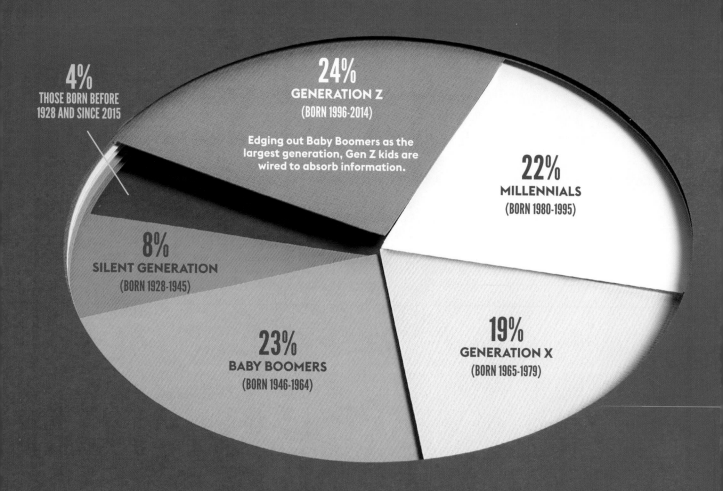

4%
THOSE BORN BEFORE 1928 AND SINCE 2015

24%
GENERATION Z
(BORN 1996-2014)

Edging out Baby Boomers as the largest generation, Gen Z kids are wired to absorb information.

22%
MILLENNIALS
(BORN 1980-1995)

8%
SILENT GENERATION
(BORN 1928-1945)

23%
BABY BOOMERS
(BORN 1946-1964)

19%
GENERATION X
(BORN 1965-1979)

information. Kids in this generation are wired to absorb information.[4] We would be wise to capitalize on this interest of things in general and help focus attention on things eternal.

If we take seriously the opportunity and impact we can have through VBS, it should recharge our batteries and motivate us to put forward our best effort. During the event we call VBS, we can help kids who feel isolated and disconnected in a virtual world—fostered by technology—find real connections with adults who know their names and are interested in the details of their lives. We can introduce them to the Savior who promises to be with them always. We can help them realize the value of spending time with others of like faith. We can connect them with a place to belong, people who care, and the transformational gospel that will positively affect the trajectory of their lives.

Since Mrs. Hawes first rented that beer parlor back in 1898, VBS has included crafts, games, music, and Bible stories as part of the daily routine. However, as Mrs. Hawes also knew, if the only place kids are exposed to biblical truth is during Bible story time, valuable time is wasted. Churches redeem the time when every element of the day—whether it's two hours, all day, for a whole week, or on the weekend—is considered a teachable moment. That's why selection of resources is vitally important. It takes time and intentionality to make sure the song lyrics, the crafts, the games, even conversations over snacks reinforce and extend learning. I've[RV] often seen a spiritual truth connect with a child during a game debrief or while working on a craft. The very nature of VBS involves all of the senses and engages every learning style. This creates an environment that allows for each child to leave knowing exactly what that day's truth was about.

For most churches, VBS is an opportunity to clearly share the gospel and introduce kids and their families to Jesus as Savior. VBS is also a significant opportunity for faith to grow. A few years ago I was privileged to visit a missionary training center. As we gathered with several of the couples who were midway through their training, we asked how God

KIDS IN THIS GENERATION ARE WIRED TO ABSORB INFORMATION. WE WOULD BE WISE TO CAPITALIZE ON THIS INTEREST OF THINGS IN GENERAL AND HELP FOCUS ATTENTION ON THINGS ETERNAL.

had brought them to this point in their lives. All of them mentioned the personal impact of VBS, either as their point of response to the gospel or as their first awareness of God's call on their lives to full-time, vocational Christian service.

Those concentrated days of VBS not only provided a platform to clearly hear the gospel, but also served to expose these future missionaries to what a life fully committed to Jesus looks like. The ripple effects of those VBS days have been carried around the world as these families were commissioned and sent to share the gospel with people everywhere.

Whether Vacation Bible School results in kids who become career missionaries, or in the planting of those first tenuous seeds of truth in young hearts—or all things in between—the "why" behind VBS doesn't change. Our primary purpose is to connect kids with Jesus. And, making those connections is worth it!

OUR PRIMARY PURPOSE IS TO CONNECT KIDS WITH JESUS.

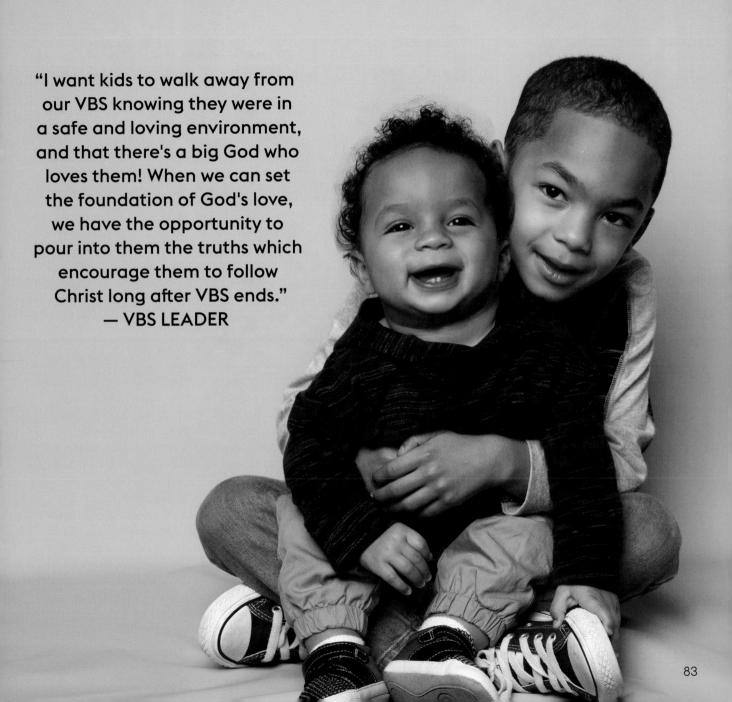

"I want kids to walk away from our VBS knowing they were in a safe and loving environment, and that there's a big God who loves them! When we can set the foundation of God's love, we have the opportunity to pour into them the truths which encourage them to follow Christ long after VBS ends."
— VBS LEADER

2 IT'S WORTH IT ... BECAUSE VBS CONNECTS KIDS WITH THE BIBLE

Sure the songs are catchy, the games are fun, and the crafts are cool, but it is called Vacation *Bible* School for a reason. We can't get all caught up with just the theme and the activities. We must remember that the heart of VBS is to connect kids in an intentional way with the Bible. That is how we truly will connect children to Jesus. Part of our mission is to let kids know that the Bible is their guide, their source for truth, and God's love letter to them through Jesus.

According to the research recorded in the book *Nothing Less*, Bible reading as child is the single greatest influence over spiritual health in young adults.[5] So if this is true, then why not capitalize on one whole week—or weekend, or time frame that fits your context—of intense Bible study for kids? Why not help kids get familiar with the Bible through a fun and engaging setting? Why not start kids off on their own path to Bible reading? Why not utilize the momentum of a concentrated time of Bible study through VBS?

23 PERCENT OF THE ADULTS WHO ATTENDED VBS AS A KID RANKED LEARNING BIBLE STORIES AS THE MOST IMPORTANT VBS ELEMENT THAT THEY REMEMBER.

Do you remember the statistic that 83 percent of parents surveyed whose child had not attended VBS say they have a positive view of Vacation Bible School overall? In addition to that research finding, we discovered that 23 percent of the adults who attended VBS as kids ranked learning Bible stories as the most important VBS element that they remember.[6] These are encouraging statistics because they say, "Yes, I want my kids to attend VBS. I see value in investing in their spiritual growth through VBS. I want them to have the same positive experiences and memories I had as a child." In these days of virtual disconnectedness, I[CT] have hope because the research shows that 69 percent of parents will encourage their kids to participate in VBS at a church they don't attend if they are invited by one of their friends. And, once the kids are here, we can connect them with the Bible.

THE NUMBER ONE PREDICTOR OF SPIRITUAL HEALTH IN YOUNG ADULTS IS CHILDHOOD BIBLE READING.

EVEN AMONG THOSE WHO DIDN'T GO TO VBS, THERE IS A STRONG BELIEF THAT VBS HELPS KIDS BETTER UNDERSTAND THE BIBLE.

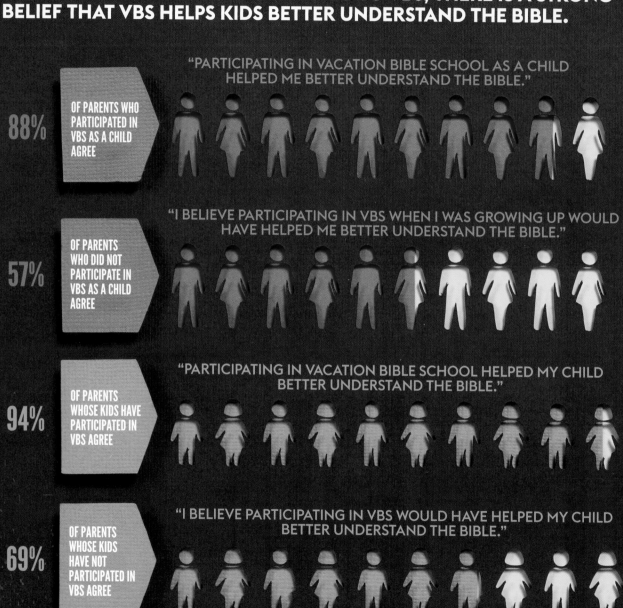

88% OF PARENTS WHO PARTICIPATED IN VBS AS A CHILD AGREE

"PARTICIPATING IN VACATION BIBLE SCHOOL AS A CHILD HELPED ME BETTER UNDERSTAND THE BIBLE."

57% OF PARENTS WHO DID NOT PARTICIPATE IN VBS AS A CHILD AGREE

"I BELIEVE PARTICIPATING IN VBS WHEN I WAS GROWING UP WOULD HAVE HELPED ME BETTER UNDERSTAND THE BIBLE."

94% OF PARENTS WHOSE KIDS HAVE PARTICIPATED IN VBS AGREE

"PARTICIPATING IN VACATION BIBLE SCHOOL HELPED MY CHILD BETTER UNDERSTAND THE BIBLE."

69% OF PARENTS WHOSE KIDS HAVE NOT PARTICIPATED IN VBS AGREE

"I BELIEVE PARTICIPATING IN VBS WOULD HAVE HELPED MY CHILD BETTER UNDERSTAND THE BIBLE."

We know that Bible reading is the number one predictor of spiritual health. And, looking at the data collected from our VBS research, clearly a vast majority of American adults—regardless of past participation in VBS—believe that VBS provides kids with a better understanding of the Bible. We also know that 23 percent of Americans surveyed have read only a few sentences or less from a Bible—ever![7] These statistics alone are enough reason to offer VBS and use this time-tested ministry to intentionally connect kids with the Bible.

God's Word instructs us to hide Scripture in our hearts and to teach it to our children. (Deuteronomy 6) We have a responsibility to teach kids that God's Word is inerrant and trustworthy. God calls us to introduce kids to the Creator and to His Son, Jesus, through Scripture. And most importantly, our job is to tell kids the good news of Jesus and His saving grace! There is a lot of pressure to ensure kids have the time to engage with the Bible in their busy lifestyles. VBS helps answer that challenge, because it can be held during just one week or one weekend!

So, just how does VBS make the Bible connect with kids? Here are some of the ways we see VBS connecting kids to their Bibles in a concentrated time of study:

- VBS connects kids with the Bible through biblically-based curriculum that is age-appropriate to ensure that biblical truths are communicated in a way kids can understand and put into practice.
- VBS connects kids to God's Word in an engaging setting that allows the gospel to speak to their hearts through the hearing of God's Word.
- VBS raises the banner for regular Bible reading and provides opportunities to support the habit of regular Bible reading in kids.
- VBS uses games, songs, crafts, and other activities to reinforce Bible teaching, using Scripture as the primary tool.
- VBS allows kids to connect Bible truths to their daily lives through life application activities.

> "EVERY BIBLE TRUTH WE SHARE, EVERY BIBLE STORY WE TELL, AND EVERY LIFE APPLICATION WE DRAW IS FOR THE POINT OF SHOWING KIDS JESUS."
>
> — BILL EMEOTT,
> LEAD MINISTRY SPECIALIST FOR LIFEWAY KIDS

It is important to note that church leaders are not alone in recognizing the importance of connecting kids with God's Word. Our latest research shows that everyone—those who attended VBS and those who haven't; those whose kids have attended and those whose kids haven't attended—agrees that VBS helps kids understand the Bible. In fact, 63 percent of Americans with a child 0–18, who identified as Christian and say they attend church regularly, want learning Bible stories to have the biggest impact on their children during a VBS event.[8] That is huge! In other words, more than the crafts they make or the songs they sing, parents want their kids to learn about Jesus through connecting with the Bible!

Since parents expect VBS to be about the Bible, and reading the Bible impacts kids' spiritual health, we need to make sure we keep *Bible* in Vacation Bible School.

"The Bible is the force that makes ministry transformational, rather than merely educational," writes Jana Magruder.[9] Therefore, VBS is the perfect ministry to connect both churched and unchurched kids with the Bible. Here are a few practical tips to help you keep the *Bible* in your VBS:

- Keep the Bible on display. Hold it while you are telling the Bible story to reinforce that you are not just telling a random story, but a true story found in the Bible.

- Make the Bible stories you share during VBS come to life. Be sure to tell the stories with emotion and inflection so that kids are interested and want to learn more.

- Provide reading plans in the materials you send home with kids. Start off by suggesting books of the Bible to read such as one of the Gospels. Encourage kids to read a few verses each day and record what they learned from the verses they read.

- Share how the Bible verses and stories you read during VBS have helped you as an adult. Remind kids that God is faithful and what He says in the Bible is true.

IF WE STRIP AWAY ALL THE SONGS AND GAMES, ALL THE CRAFTS AND FUN, VBS IS AT ITS VERY CORE A TIME TO CONNECT KIDS WITH THE BIBLE AND THE TRUTHS WRITTEN WITHIN IT.

63% OF CHRISTIAN PARENTS WHO ATTEND CHURCH REGULARLY SAY THEY WANT LEARNING BIBLE STORIES TO HAVE THE BIGGEST IMPACT ON THEIR CHILD DURING A VBS EVENT.

AMONG AMERICAN PARENTS WHO SAY THEY DO NOT HAVE A CHILD WHO HAS ATTENDED VBS:

71%

AGREE THAT PARTICIPATING IN VBS WOULD HAVE DIRECTLY IMPACTED THEIR CHILD'S SPIRITUAL GROWTH IN POSITIVE WAYS

42%

SAY THEY RECALL OTHER FAMILIES WHO HAD PARTICIPATED IN VBS TALKING ABOUT LEARNING BIBLE STORIES

28%

RANKED LEARNING BIBLE STORIES FIRST AMONG THE VBS ELEMENTS THAT SEEMED THE MOST IMPORTANT TO FAMILIES WHO PARTICIPATED IN VBS

AMONG AMERICAN PARENTS WHO SAY THEY HAVE A CHILD WHO HAS ATTENDED VBS:

49%

RECALL THEIR CHILD TALKING ABOUT LEARNING BIBLE STORIES AFTER PARTICIPATING IN VBS

40%

RANKED LEARNING BIBLE STORIES ONE OF THE TOP THREE ELEMENTS THEIR CHILD TALKED ABOUT AFTER PARTICIPATING IN VBS

AMONG ADULTS WHO DID NOT ATTEND VBS AS A CHILD,

36% REMEMBER OTHER KIDS TALKING ABOUT LEARNING BIBLE STORIES

- Provide opportunities to use Bible dictionaries, concordances, commentaries, and age-appropriate apps as part of your Bible skills activities.
- Incrementally introduce Bible skills that individual children can grasp, based on their age.
- Encourage kids to read their Bibles during VBS in order to give them confidence to read their Bibles at home.

The Bible is the key to connecting kids to Jesus as their Savior and Lord. It is their guide, their source of hope, and ultimately the one place they can turn for absolute truth. VBS leads kids to start down a path of studying their Bibles and growing in their relationship with Jesus. If we strip away all the songs and games, all the crafts and fun, VBS is at its very core a time to connect kids with the Bible and the truths written within it. And that alone makes VBS worth it!

"SO MY WORD THAT COMES FROM MY MOUTH WILL NOT RETURN TO ME EMPTY, BUT IT WILL ACCOMPLISH WHAT I PLEASE AND WILL PROSPER IN WHAT I SEND IT TO DO."

ISAIAH 55:11

3 IT'S WORTH IT ... BECAUSE VBS CONNECTS KIDS WITH REAL LIFE

Today is a different world than what I[CP] grew up in. We did not have cell phones and social media. The Internet was new. I was in college before I had an email address. My computer was huge and tied to a desk. If I wanted to talk to my friends, I called them on a landline or wrote letters. Today's kids don't know what it's like not to instantly receive replies from friends. Even toddlers know how to work phones and electronic tablets to watch videos and play games. All of this technology has changed the way kids see the world, how they learn, and how they interact with others.

Kids live in a virtual world of social media and video games. They can sit at home and talk to people all over the world through games and various apps. Therefore, many kids lack the social skills they need to be successful in life. Vacation Bible School is a real-life experience where kids can come and learn more about the Bible in community.

Our research shows that 83 percent of people who attended VBS as children agree that participating in VBS was one of their most meaningful church experiences.[10] Why? There could be several reasons. At VBS, children experience church in a more relaxed atmosphere and meet new people. They know they are there to learn and have fun—lots of fun! Kids may be in rooms that are normally set aside for adult classes. It is fun to explore new areas of the church building! Also, kids get to interact with adults they don't normally see as part of their routine church experience.

These real-time relationships are important. Sadly, today's kids are literal thinkers living in a virtual world. Many spend their time in front of the computer instead of playing with friends. Kids love games like Minecraft where they can build their own worlds and control what happens.

Electronic games are fun and use the imagination, but we need to ensure that kids grow up knowing the Bible is about real people and a real God. The stories in the Bible are not fiction designed to entertain us. During

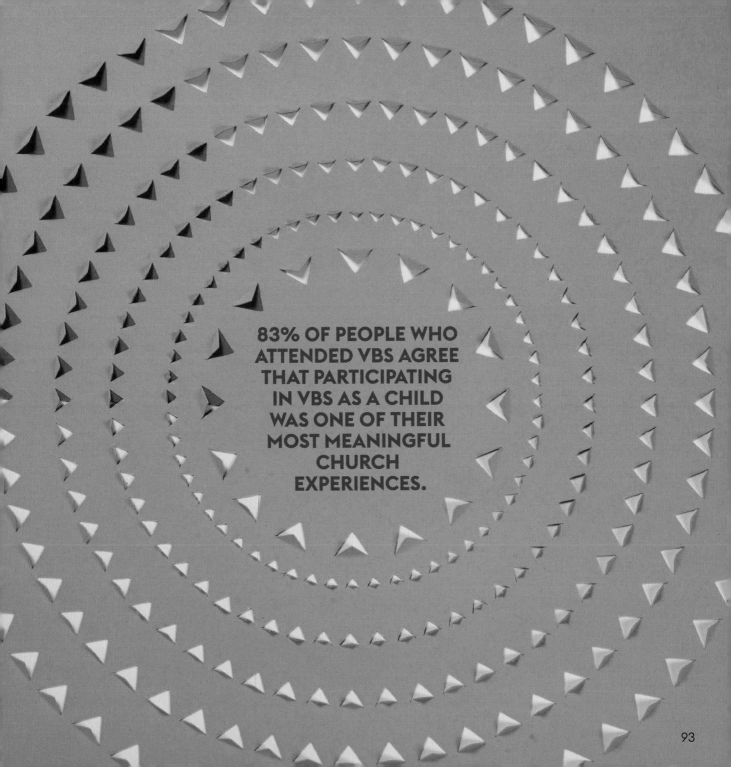

83% OF PEOPLE WHO ATTENDED VBS AGREE THAT PARTICIPATING IN VBS AS A CHILD WAS ONE OF THEIR MOST MEANINGFUL CHURCH EXPERIENCES.

"Children who feel connected and loved, valued and appreciated, can begin to see and understand who God is, how Jesus cared for and loved them by his sacrifice, and will be more receptive to the message of the gospel."
—VBS LEADER

VBS, kids will learn with other kids in real time about the One True God and how they can know and follow Him.

Kids in Gen Z (kids born in 1996–2014) are accustomed to listening to someone talk while they are simultaneously checking social media and playing video games. We don't always think they are paying attention, but usually they are even if they are not looking at us. They live their lives out on social media, where others are watching everything they do. Therefore, it is even more important that we know their language, what they're watching, and how to connect with them in life and at church.[11]

If we want to connect kids with real-life experiences, we first must acknowledge that technology is not a bad thing. In fact, we can use technology as a tool to engage kids in learning the Bible. Many kids are bringing mobile phones to church with Bible apps instead of physical Bibles. If that is how they want to read the Bible, then encourage them, especially if they are preteens. These kids may need more help learning how to navigate their Bible app. Also, we can show kids how to use physical Bibles in order to develop Bible skills transferable to any device. Furthermore, some apps include Bible reference tools that enhance the Bible-learning process, facilitating the transference of Bible exploration from the church to the home.

I[LH] wonder if the adults who taught you and me when we were children bemoaned the fact that our world was different than the one they grew up in? Chances are, they did to some extent. My granddad had a saying—human nature has never changed. That is a biblical truth. We are all born with a sin nature. However, what has changed is the world in which kids live. The real world of today's kids is unlike the real world you and I experienced as children. The same could be said of our parents' and grandparents' generations. Nevertheless just as our teachers and leaders did, you and I must adapt our methods—not our message—to reach the kids of every generation. That's why we connect a real Bible about a real Jesus to real kids, and it's worth it!

WE NEED TO ENSURE THAT KIDS GROW UP KNOWING THE BIBLE IS ABOUT REAL PEOPLE AND A REAL GOD.

4 IT'S WORTH IT ... BECAUSE VBS CONNECTS KIDS WITH ADULTS

My[LH] earliest memory of VBS is a brief, visual snapshot. As a preschooler, I'm standing outside Second Baptist Church, Corpus Christi, Texas, with my dad, the associate pastor. I'm too young to go inside when the other children soon will begin marching into the worship center, so my dad gives me a VBS attendance pin before attending to his duties as the VBS Director. That's it. That's all I remember. But, the memory is forever imprinted in my mind.

What is your VBS story? Are you among the 60 percent of adults who attended VBS while growing up? Do you have fond memories of those VBS days? If so, you're in the majority—9 out of 10 American adults who attended VBS while growing up report having positive memories of those experiences. And, if you did attend VBS, chances are you went because your immediate family, relatives, neighbors, or friends took you or invited you.[12]

That's the story of the young mother who taught VBS with me this past summer. As we met to begin planning to teach six- and seven-year-olds, I discovered that my co-teacher's primary memory of VBS was as a child about that same age. Her family did not attend an evangelical church, and a friend invited her to VBS one year. I enjoyed mentoring this new teacher and observing her enthusiastic engagement with boys and girls.

To make our week even more serendipitous, one of the girls in our Bible study group had a similar church background as my co-teacher. When I tried to explain the Trinity (I'm not sure what I was thinking when I stumbled into *that* conversation with rising second graders!), this young girl very seriously tried to help my already-awkward explanation by showing me how to make the sign of the cross. There it was. Another brief snapshot. Three generations relating to one another, engaging in Bible conversation.

CHANCES ARE YOU WENT TO VBS BECAUSE YOUR IMMEDIATE FAMILY, RELATIVES, NEIGHBORS, OR FRIENDS TOOK YOU OR INVITED YOU.

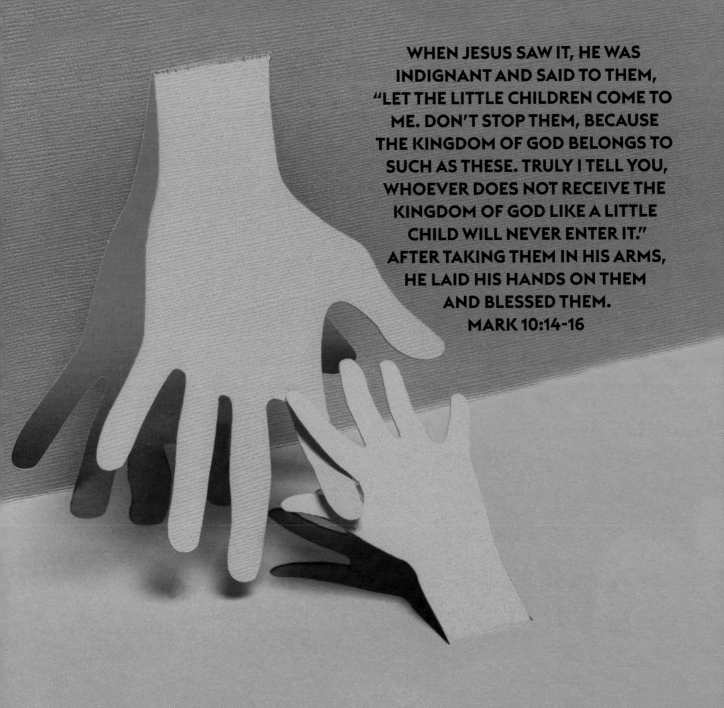

WHEN JESUS SAW IT, HE WAS INDIGNANT AND SAID TO THEM, "LET THE LITTLE CHILDREN COME TO ME. DON'T STOP THEM, BECAUSE THE KINGDOM OF GOD BELONGS TO SUCH AS THESE. TRULY I TELL YOU, WHOEVER DOES NOT RECEIVE THE KINGDOM OF GOD LIKE A LITTLE CHILD WILL NEVER ENTER IT." AFTER TAKING THEM IN HIS ARMS, HE LAID HIS HANDS ON THEM AND BLESSED THEM.
MARK 10:14-16

DIFFICULTY RECRUITING TEACHERS AND VOLUNTEERS IS THE NUMBER ONE REASON CHURCHES CHOOSE NOT TO HOST A VBS.

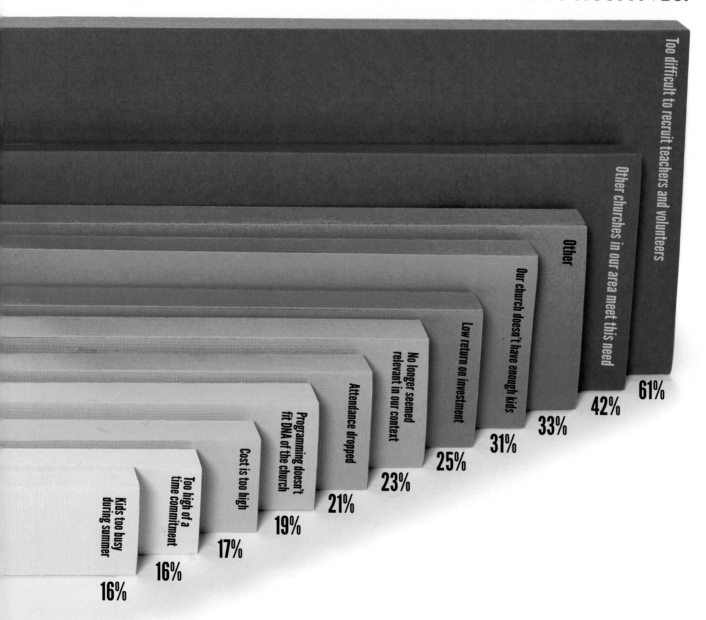

Too difficult to recruit teachers and volunteers — 61%

Other churches in our area meet this need — 42%

Other — 33%

Our church doesn't have enough kids — 31%

Low return on investment — 25%

No longer seemed relevant in our context — 23%

Attendance dropped — 21%

Programming doesn't fit DNA of the church — 19%

Cost is too high — 17%

Too high of a time commitment — 16%

Kids too busy during summer — 16%

My experience this summer is not unlike what happens every week in thousands of churches, impacting millions of kids. According to LifeWay's *Nothing Less* research, one of the 15 influencers of an individual's spiritual health is the connections a child makes "with several adults at church who intentionally invested in them." Another way to look at this is, "a child who connected with several adults at church who intentionally invested in her spiritually and personally while growing up has 3.75 percent stronger spiritual health as a young adult."[13]

In our most recent research, we discovered that among American adults who attended VBS growing up, 30 percent indicate learning from teachers and volunteers is one of their strongest memories of VBS. Knowing this, I invite you to join me in leaping to a conclusion. Of churches that did not conduct VBS in the last three to five years, 61 percent say they didn't host a VBS because it was too difficult to recruit teachers and volunteers.[14] If this fact is true—and it is certainly a prevalent perception—then the decision not to conduct VBS may deprive a child from engaging with the one adult who would've introduced him or her to Jesus. Now, I realize that I just made several assumptions, but can we afford to gamble with the lives of kids when eternity is at stake?

Let's not underestimate the value of kids and adults connecting at VBS, regardless of whether or not those children impact the church's future attendance records. "The relationships and connections that are made during an event like this are crucial. Even if the family or child never returns, the impact that was made for the Kingdom should be memorable," states one VBS leader.[15]

We should follow Jesus' example when He said, "Let the little children come to me. Don't stop them, because the kingdom of God belongs to such as these." (Mark 10:14) In this brief encounter, Jesus showed us the importance of connecting kids with adults. In a gentle, personal moment, "after taking them in his arms, he [Jesus] laid his hands on them and blessed them." (Mark 10:16) Jesus demonstrated—they're worth it.

AMONG AMERICAN ADULTS WHO ATTENDED VBS GROWING UP, 30% INDICATE LEARNING FROM TEACHERS AND VOLUNTEERS IS ONE OF THEIR STRONGEST MEMORIES OF VBS.

"THE RELATIONSHIPS AND CONNECTIONS THAT ARE MADE DURING AN EVENT LIKE THIS ARE CRUCIAL."
—VBS LEADER

5 IT'S WORTH IT ... BECAUSE VBS CONNECTS TEENS WITH SERVICE

In his letter to Timothy, Paul affirmed his protégé as a spiritual leader and an example to others, in spite of his young age. Whenever I[MT] hear children and teenagers referred to as "the church of tomorrow," my heart sinks. They are not the next generation church; they are the church of today! A vibrant, integral part of the body of Christ. Rather than waiting until he got older, Paul encouraged Timothy to embrace his role of servant leadership immediately. Oh that we could all be like Paul and see the value each and every member brings to the body!

Teens don't have to wait until they are fully grown to begin serving in the church. The earlier they get started, the better! Research conducted in 2007 and 2016 indicates that children who regularly served in church while growing up are more spiritually healthy and less likely to drop out of church once they reach young adulthood than their peers who did not serve in church.[16] The more teens see themselves as an integral part of the body of Christ, the more likely they are to stay connected, and to keep serving.

This presents the church with an incredible opportunity. We have the potential to actually impact the future by offering teens opportunities to serve today. Of course, this requires work on our part to make sure teens are well equipped, well trained, and able to take on the responsibility of sharing the gospel with kids. But, it is an opportunity we cannot afford to miss!

Serving is an essential part of discipleship. It is a mature expression of one's obedience, love, and followship of Christ. When we serve God and serve others, we are offering to God a spiritual act of worship. Jesus repeatedly modeled the importance of service as He humbled Himself and became a servant. Through serving, God refashions us to become more like His Son, which makes service an essential component of

DON'T LET ANYONE DESPISE YOUR YOUTH, BUT SET AN EXAMPLE FOR THE BELIEVERS IN SPEECH, IN CONDUCT, IN LOVE, IN FAITH, AND IN PURITY.

I TIMOTHY 4:12

TWO SEPARATE STUDIES HAVE SHOWN THE BENEFITS OF CONNECTING TEENS WITH SERVING IN CHURCH.

16%

16% MORE YOUNG ADULTS WHO REMAINED IN CHURCH HAD REGULAR RESPONSIBILITIES WITHIN THE CHURCH THAN THOSE WHO DROPPED OUT.

7.5%

KIDS WHO REGULARLY SERVED IN CHURCH HAD 7.5% STRONGER SPIRITUAL HEALTH AS YOUNG ADULTS.

SERVING IS AN
ESSENTIAL PART
OF DISCIPLESHIP.
IT IS A MATURE
EXPRESSION OF
ONE'S OBEDIENCE,
LOVE, AND
FOLLOWSHIP OF
CHRIST.

spiritual growth. Like all spiritual disciplines, service requires practice in order to make it a habit. And, VBS provides a great practice field for teens.

VBS is an easy "first serve" for students. It's a natural fit! Often, serving in VBS is viewed as a type of rite of passage. Kids grow up going to VBS as participants, and then once they age out of it they begin to serve in VBS. Many teens have a deep love for VBS and are happy to have a way to still be involved. Teenagers bring energy and enthusiasm to VBS and are often the key in helping preteens stay engaged. An older teen guy can make VBS activities seem cool to a fifth or sixth grade boy!

Teenagers are capable of so much more than just being "helpers" at VBS! They crave real responsibility and thrive when the bar is set high. In my experience, people will almost always rise to whatever expectation is set for them. Case in point, I once took a group of 7th and 8th graders on a mission trip to do VBS. As we met together to plan ahead of the trip, I explained that in the eyes of the children we would teach, these teens would be their teachers—the authority figures, the "grown ups." We talked together about the important work of sharing the gospel and how everything they did and said on this trip would either point people to or away from Christ.

Every single one of these teens bought into the vision and embraced the seriousness of the work before them. They embraced their roles as teachers and led small group activities each day. Before the trip, I wondered if the responsibility would be too great or if I was asking too much of them. Not at all. They shone in their roles! And what's more, every single one of them returned to do it again with me the next year. And the year after that, and the year after that—all the way to graduation. They thrived as teachers. They excelled as leaders. They loved the responsibility—they couldn't get enough of it!

Teens are hungry for meaningful work and ready to tackle any challenge we can throw at them—even the "non-glamorous" aspects of VBS. During the course of this research study, several church leaders spoke about

"The key for getting all kids to try all things is our teenage counselors who participate right alongside the kids."
— VBS LEADER

"We have more volunteers than we need, but our teens want to be a part of VBS and especially the week before when we are preparing—so we use them all! We spend the week with them learning to serve. ... They have amazing ideas, creativity, and unending energy. They feel a huge sense of ownership about our VBS."
— VBS LEADER

the value of teens serving in the weeks of preparation leading up to VBS. Teenagers approach even the mundane tasks of preparing leader pack items, setting up the room, or writing names on name tags with enthusiasm and creativity. Helping with these aspects of VBS—rather than just showing up at start-time on day one—helps teens develop a sense of ownership. They get an idea of the amount of work that goes into making VBS happen and can bring a needed burst of energy to get the work done. If we let them, they will also bring their own fresh ideas to the table. Granted they may not know everything yet, but who does? We can help students be successful by allowing experienced VBS leaders to serve as mentors to teen leaders.

Teenagers are like sponges ready to soak up the wisdom and experience of the leaders with whom they are paired. Many are eager to learn anything we will teach them. For example, they probably do not know that removing a few pieces from a puzzle actually encourages a young child to want to work the puzzle, or that intentionally putting those pieces to the left of the puzzle helps develop pre-reading skills. They may not realize that recreation games can be used to teach Bible truths. They may not know how to use conversation to capitalize on a teaching moment. But they can certainly learn how to do all of those things!

By serving alongside seasoned leaders as equals, not just as "helpers," students can learn to serve with excellence and develop new skills that will allow them to serve in children's ministry—or wherever God calls them to serve—for the rest of their lives. So, let's invest in teens and connect them to service—it will be worth it!

6 IT'S WORTH IT ... BECAUSE VBS CONNECTS EVERYONE

What would you do if you had one week to totally throw yourself into learning a new skill or honing one you already have? For five days, you did nothing but that one thing. Would you devote your time to exercising, traveling, fishing, or shopping? What if you chose to devote it to learning about God and studying His Word? Just imagine what you could learn in five days! That is what happens during Vacation Bible School.

During VBS, we have the opportunity to host kids, teens, and adults in our churches for five days in a row. We can fill them with the love of Jesus and help them to grow and learn more on their own. How often does this happen in your church? Probably only once a year! VBS is the one ministry that has the potential to connect everyone in the church with the gospel.

That connection is possible because, for the most part, VBS occurs over consecutive days for a concentrated period of time. Why is this important? Our research suggests that a child who is considered actively involved in church may actually only attend church one to two times a month, which translates into a couple of hours each month. A traditional VBS involves three hours a day for five days in a row. If you total it up, VBS results in 15 hours of intense discipleship, the gospel being shared daily, and 7 months' worth of ministry in 1 week. The opportunities for evangelism, discipleship, and relationship-building that can take place in one week of VBS might take half a year for a Sunday School teacher.[17]

We know that sometimes it can be hit or miss with kids coming to Sunday School or other weekly church activities, but VBS is an event that kids look forward to each year; therefore, it is one they want to come to every day. Kids enjoy being able to come to church and learn with kids their own age. Whether they act like it or not, kids also cherish relationships with teen and adult leaders and teachers. Many kids even share the experience with their friends, inviting and bringing them to VBS. As one church leader

THE OPPORTUNITIES FOR EVANGELISM, DISCIPLESHIP, AND RELATIONSHIP BUILDING THAT CAN TAKE PLACE IN ONE WEEK OF VBS MIGHT TAKE HALF A YEAR FOR A SUNDAY SCHOOL TEACHER.

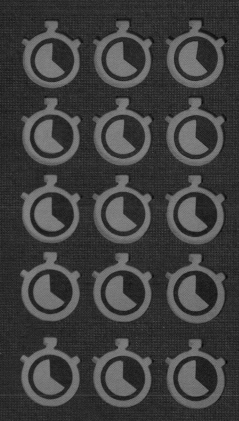

CURRENT RESEARCH SUGGESTS THAT A CHILD WHO IS ACTIVELY INVOLVED IN CHURCH MAY ACTUALLY ONLY ATTEND CHURCH **1–2 TIMES A MONTH,** WHICH TRANSLATES INTO **A COUPLE OF HOURS EACH MONTH.**

A TRADITIONAL VBS INVOLVES **3 HOURS A DAY FOR 5 DAYS IN A ROW.** THIS IS EQUIVALENT TO **7 MONTHS OF "CHURCH"** FOR TODAY'S TYPICAL, CHURCHGOING CHILD!

15 HOURS

GOSPEL BEING SHARED

7 MONTHS

IN ONE WEEK

IF YOU TOTAL IT UP, VBS RESULTS IN

15 HOURS OF INTENSE DISCIPLESHIP,

THE GOSPEL BEING SHARED DAILY,

AND **7 MONTHS** OF MINISTRY IN **1 WEEK.**

put it, "VBS is an intense week with a chunk of ministry in a short amount of time. Relationships are built during the time and kids are exposed to truth for lots of hours."[18]

Investing in five concentrated days—or in a weekend—allows teachers and volunteers an opportunity to get to know kids and build relationships with them. Spending three hours a day with a child for five days in a row helps a teacher know the child beyond the "good morning" and "see you next week" of a weekly church activity. As teachers teach the Bible study and go to the different rotations with kids, time is available for conversation and questions. These conversations are not forced, and they can lead to Kingdom-impacting questions. The more comfortable a child feels around an adult, the more likely he is to ask deeper questions that he might have felt embarrassed to ask previously.

Another benefit to ministering to kids over a period of consecutive days is found in the concept of repetition. We know that repetition is one way kids learn. How many times have you tried to encourage kids in your ministry to learn a Bible verse? You teach it to them one week, then when they come back the next week, you feel as though you are starting over because they have forgotten the verse. During a concentrated weekend or week of Bible study, you can teach kids the verse on the first day. Chances are good they will be back the very next day to continue learning. You'll have the opportunity to not only help them find the verse in their Bibles, but memorize it, understand what the verse means, and apply it to their lives. Coming back the next day and reinforcing what they learned the day before helps kids be more successful in Bible learning.

It's worth repeating an earlier quote, "VBS is unique in that it provides a concentrated dose of biblical teaching to our own children, as well as the opportunity to reach the lost in our community with the gospel of Christ."[19] The heart of VBS is sharing the good news of Jesus Christ. For one solid week everyone can hear the gospel every single day. It's a worthwhile investment with eternal significance.

FOR ONE SOLID WEEK EVERYONE CAN HEAR THE GOSPEL EVERY SINGLE DAY. IT'S A WORTHWHILE INVESTMENT WITH ETERNAL SIGNIFICANCE.

4

IT'S WORTH IT ...
BECAUSE ETERNITY
IS WORTH IT

1 VBS BUSTS THE MYTHS

You've made it this far. You understand the crisis. You agree that sharing the gospel is worth it. But, quite frankly, you still have some resistance. You keep thinking of those "Yes, but ... " statements that people are quick to toss your way when the subject of VBS is mentioned. Let's talk about the elephant in the room and call these myths (or excuses) on the carpet.

MYTH #1: People are just using us for free childcare.

First, according to LifeWay Research, only 12 percent of parents say they are interested in VBS as a form of inexpensive childcare.[1] So if 60 families participate in your VBS, only 7 of those families chose your VBS for free childcare. However, the good news is—THEY CAME! The parents are willing for their kids to be there and to hear what you have to teach them. They trust your church enough to bring their kids. Some may begin to attend your church and worship with you. Every summer we hear stories of kids who came to VBS and, before the week ended, one of their parents trusted Jesus as Savior.

On the other hand, some may not return until next year's VBS. Be patient. Plant seeds. Trust God for the increase. Think of it this way—even if you are just getting this one chance to plant the message of the gospel in a child's heart, isn't it worth it? "Let the little children come!" (Mark 10:14)

MYTH #2: We don't have enough workers. No one volunteers.

This is usually a great time to step back and look at two things. First, how are you structuring your VBS? How many key leaders do you have? What would a VBS designed with just those leaders in position look like? Then begin to incorporate less experienced leaders and teenagers as "leaders in training."

Second, how are you enlisting them? "All call" announcements rarely work. Ask God to point out people to you, then ask them one-on-one. Give them

EVEN IF YOU ARE JUST GETTING THIS ONE CHANCE TO PLANT THE MESSAGE OF THE GOSPEL IN A CHILD'S HEART, ISN'T IT WORTH IT?

ONLY **12%** OF PARENTS CITED CHILDCARE AS A FACTOR THAT CONTRIBUTED TO THEIR CHILDREN PARTICIPATING IN VBS.

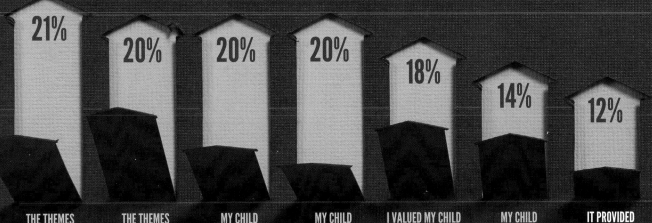

21%	20%	20%	20%	18%	14%	12%
THE THEMES WERE APPEALING TO MY CHILD	THE THEMES WERE APPEALING TO ME	MY CHILD VALUED THEIR SPIRITUAL GROWTH	MY CHILD VALUED STUDYING THE BIBLE	I VALUED MY CHILD BUILDING RELATIONSHIPS WITH OTHERS IN THE CHURCH	MY CHILD VALUED BUILDING RELATIONSHIPS WITH OTHERS IN THE CHURCH	IT PROVIDED ME WITH AN INEXPENSIVE CHILDCARE OPTION

*Reasons why parents chose to bring their kids to VBS

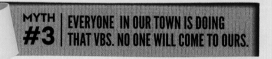

79% OF RESPONDENTS DISAGREE WITH THE STATEMENT "PARENTS IN OUR CHURCH COMPLAIN WHEN OUR VBS IS THE SAME AS OTHER CHURCHES IN THE AREA"

21%
AGREE

79%
DISAGREE

AND 78% OF LEADERS DISAGREE WHEN ASKED WHETHER KIDS COMPLAIN.

simple but clear expectations of the role and give them time to think and pray (but set a deadline for an answer). I[RV] have lost count of the times I've asked someone to help teach and received a fearful or skeptical response. But, if God led me to that person, I honestly can't remember a single time they said, "Never again!" In fact the responses have been, "Thank you so much! I had no idea I'd enjoy it that much!" or "Put me down for next year if I can be with the same age group." And many, many times those same people eventually became part of the faithful ongoing team of teachers in other areas of kids ministry.

MYTH #3: Every church in town is doing that VBS. No one will come to ours. (or "We want to be different." or "We want to stand out.")

LifeWay research shows that Research found that 79 percent of parents have no problem with a VBS theme being the same as other churches, nor did 78 percent of kids.[2] Usually the problem is the perception of either the leadership or, possibly, the volunteers.

Maybe, the solution involves just a bit of rethinking. Kids learn best through repetition. Kids never tire of singing songs they love. (Ask parents who live with the VBS music blaring in their car all summer!) Except for the sign out front, your VBS will be unique to you because the people leading it are different. And, not to be flippant, but there are no new Bible stories. However, we are teaching from God's Word which is "living and effective and sharper than any double-edged sword." (Hebrews 4:12) Trust the Master Teacher, God's Spirit, to equip your teachers. If you've taught kids for very long, you know you can tell a Bible story for the 100th time and suddenly you'll see the light go on! It is the coolest thing! That child may have heard the story at the church across town last week, but today you are there to witness when the seed takes root!

MYTH #4: VBS is too expensive! We have to buy too much stuff.

When I go to the grocery store to buy food for my family, I don't buy everything on the shelves. However, everything on the shelves is bought by *someone*. That's because our needs and preferences are different. VBS

WHAT IF NO ONE
COMES BUT
"OUR CHURCH
KIDS?"
AREN'T THEY
WORTH IT?

resource providers are like those grocery stores, making every effort to provide everything *someone* needs. By the same token, just because it's cheaper doesn't mean it's better. I have learned the hard way that there are a few grocery items that will go to waste if they are less desirable. The better brand is worth it.

Trustworthy VBS resources should do more than just pick five Bible stories. The content should be carefully crafted to share the gospel and help kids grow in their faith. Once you've selected the resources with the content you feel best meets that criteria, then decide what other elements are most important to you. Snacks, crafts, and decorations can be areas to look for savings either through donations or adaptations.

MYTH #5: The only kids who come are our church kids.

According to LifeWay Research, children's ministry leaders indicate that VBS attendance consistently is double any other ongoing kids ministry. About half attending VBS are not kids from that church—29 percent attend another church and the rest of the kids (fully 22 percent) do not attend church at all.[3] So, in most cases those who attend your VBS will be both regular attending church kids and guests.

But, I have to get on my soapbox about this misconception for just a moment. What if no one comes but "our church kids?" Aren't they worth it? God has placed those kids in our church. If we send the message they're not worth the trouble, could this result in attitudes when they're older that church is not worth the trouble? What does VBS do for the kids who call your church "home?" It tells them you value them. You care about their spiritual growth. You believe God's plans for them so much, you want them to have an experience that says, "Our church thinks you are worth it!" We want them to experience Christian fellowship that is fun and Bible study that is valuable.

Ok, I'll climb down off my soapbox and get back to the question of "other" kids coming. Can we just be honest here? Over the years I've seen our churches spend lots of money paying for ads, handing out scores of flyers,

51%

CHURCH LEADERS REPORT THAT THEY AVERAGE 51% UNCHURCHED KIDS OR KIDS FROM OTHER CHURCHES AT VBS.

49% OF VBS PARTICIPANTS ATTEND THEIR OWN CHURCH

29% ATTEND OTHER CHURCHES

22% DO NOT ATTEND CHURCH

putting up signs, and bombarding social media. But, hands down, the most effective way to get kids to VBS is when "our" kids invite their friends (or when VBS volunteers bring kids from their families or neighborhoods). Don't forget, one of our strongest takeaways from LifeWay's VBS research is that 69 percent of parents said they would encourage their child to participate in a VBS event at a church they don't attend *if invited by one of their friends.*[4]

MYTH #6: All our kids are already Christians. VBS is not about discipleship.

A disciple is "one who learns from another." Consider these VBS discipleship opportunities:

- Kids who are already Christians affirm their faith. Each time believers review the plan of salvation, their foundation of faith is strengthened and they are better equipped to share that message with others.
- Bible study is a key component of discipleship. During VBS, participants of all ages are tutored in using their Bibles and challenged to make Bible reading a part of their daily lives.
- Leaders mentor new leaders. Training up future leaders is discipleship!
- Kids get to know Christian adults and learn from them how important following God is in their lives.
- Remember what we said in chapter two? The Great Commission tells us to "Disciple!" Teaching, sharing the gospel, and helping kids know more about Jesus is true discipleship.

The bottom line is we have a choice. We can believe the myths and make the excuses. We can plan lots of social events and field trips and fill calendars. Building relationships is important. But, if we fail to make an effort to reach people with the gospel, then that fail is eternal. Is VBS the only way? No. But it is one way that has a proven track record. It is flexible enough to change with the times, yet focused enough to deliver a consistent message. It is worth it!

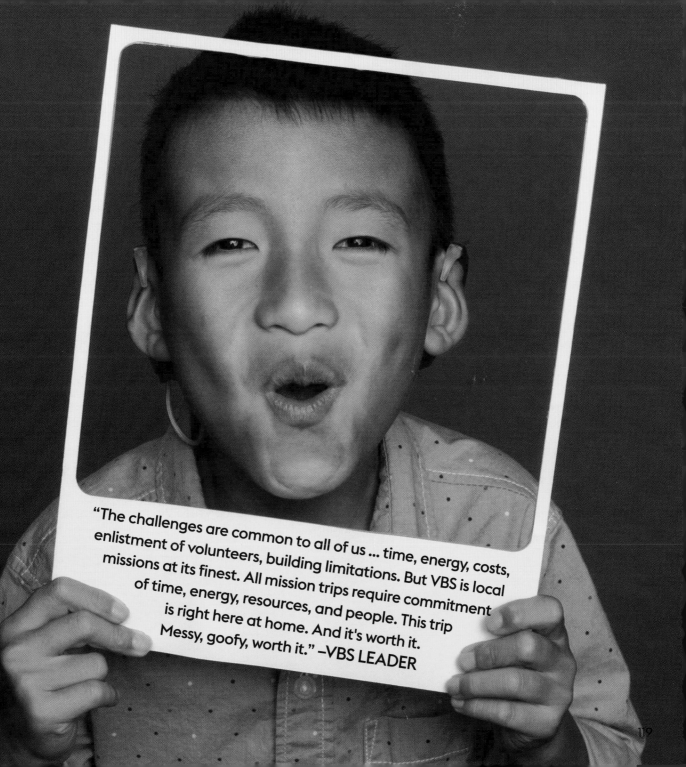

"The challenges are common to all of us ... time, energy, costs, enlistment of volunteers, building limitations. But VBS is local missions at its finest. All mission trips require commitment of time, energy, resources, and people. This trip is right here at home. And it's worth it. Messy, goofy, worth it." –VBS LEADER

2 VBS IMPACTS THE FUTURE

In the previous chapter, I mentioned my visual snapshot of a much younger Landry standing on the sidewalk with my dad before the VBS day officially commenced. Several years later, another memory was captured on actual film when, as a 16-year-old, I carried my glass beehive to VBS and talked to a group of children about God's busy, buzzing creatures. Two snapshots. Two memories. Two examples of the importance of connecting kids, teens, and adults with the gospel.

But, is it really worth it? Is VBS just a program with a long legacy that needs to be put out to the proverbial pasture? Instead of the encouraging whisper, "build it and he will come," the enemy often whispers the opposite.

As you cut 50 pieces of construction paper, the enemy whispers, "Is it worth it?"

After you burn yourself with hot glue, the enemy whispers, "Is it worth it?"

When the three-year-old with authority issues punches and kicks you, the enemy whispers, "Is it worth it?"

When the seven-year-old has a meltdown on the last day of VBS, the enemy whispers, "Is it worth it?"

As you reassure the stressed-out preteen that she is made in God's image, the enemy whispers, "Is it worth it?"

When the alarm goes off at five in the morning on the third day of VBS and you know what's waiting for you at the office in the afternoon, the enemy whispers, "Is it worth it?"

When I directed my first VBS as a young seminary graduate, my dad told me, "Your first VBS as a church staff member may be your best because you'll lead it by the book." He was correct, it was my best VBS experience. But, I definitely had my "Is it worth it?" moments that summer. My wife was six months pregnant with our first child, and I was in the middle of radiation treatments for cancer. VBS couldn't have come at a worse time, yet God showed me that my first VBS 30 years ago—and every VBS I've participated in since then—was worth it.

What about you? What is your answer? Before you respond, think back on the statistics and stories in the pages of this book. For more than 120 years, God has used VBS to impact the eternity of millions of people, all over the globe. If we stop using VBS as a tool for evangelism and discipleship, where will our churches be 10, 20, 30 years from now? Knowing that 22 percent of children who participate in VBS do not attend any church, what will take the place of VBS to reach kids and families for the sake of the gospel?[5] VBS is not a program to save, it's a ministry tool with a future. My prayer and the prayer of everyone who worked on this book is that when faced with the question, "Is it worth it?" we'll all clearly hear, "Yes, it's worth it, because eternity is worth it."

IF WE STOP USING VBS AS A TOOL FOR EVANGELISM AND DISCIPLESHIP, WHERE WILL OUR CHURCHES BE 10, 20, 30 YEARS FROM NOW?

END NOTES

CONTRIBUTING AUTHORS

BETHANY BROWN[BB] served as Copy Editor for *It's Worth It*. She wrote "The Solution is Timeless" and "Because VBS Works." She serves as Production Editor on LifeWay's VBS team. Bethany grew up as a missionary kid in Tanzania. She has taken a variety of roles in her church's Backyard Kids Club near Nashville.

GORDON BROWN[GB] wrote "Mobilizes to Reach." He serves as Graphic Designer on LifeWay's VBS team. Gordon teaches preschoolers in VBS and children's choir at his church in Nashville.

ISAAC KIERSTEAD[IK] wrote "VBS Energizes." He serves as Graphic Designer on LifeWay's VBS team. Isaac serves in a variety of kids ministry roles including large group teacher at VBS and part-time children's director.

JANA MAGRUDER[JM] wrote the "Introduction" and "Churches and Individuals are in Crisis." She serves as Director of Kids Ministry for LifeWay Christian Resources.

CANDACE POWELL[CP] wrote "Connects Kids with Real Life" and Connects Everyone." She serves as Content Editor for Kids on LifeWay's VBS team. Candace teaches preteen Sunday School and a variety of roles in VBS at her church near Springfield, Tennessee.

KLISTA STORTS[KS] wrote "Mobilizes to Teach" and "Relates to Parents." She serves as Content Editor for Preschool on LifeWay's VBS team and has long been involved in leadership training. Klista teaches preschool VBS at her church near Nashville.

MELITA THOMAS[MT] wrote "VBS Attracts," "Mobilizes to Lead," and "Connects Teens with Service." She serves as the VBS Ministry Specialist for LifeWay. Melita teaches kindergartners in both VBS and Sunday School and works with preteens in choir at her church in Nashville.

CAROL TOMLINSON[CT] wrote "Connects Kids with the Bible." She serves as Content Editor for Preteen, Student, and Adult on LifeWay's VBS team. Carol serves as VBS director and works with students at her church in Smyrna, Tennessee.

RHONDA VANCLEAVE[RV] served as General Editor for *It's Worth It*. She wrote "VBS Is About Jesus," "Connects Kids with Jesus," and "VBS Busts the Myths." She serves as Publishing Team Leader for LifeWay's VBS team. Rhonda has been in kids ministry for more than 40 years. She is VBS director at her church in Columbia, Tennessee.

ENDORSEMENTS

"Summer time can mean long unstructured days for many children. VBS gives kids and parents a time to come together with the community to learn about the Bible in an age-appropriate and engaging way. It's a great way for the church to be a beacon within the community."

–DR. DERWIN L. GRAY
Pastor, Transformation Church

"When a church of hundreds was asked when they accepted Jesus as Savior, the number one answer was VBS. I was there and that moment sealed the deal for the rest of my life."

–LEITH ANDERSON
President, National Association of Evangelicals

"While growing up, VBS played a huge role in helping shape me as a follower of Christ. I think it is an underutilized asset in helping establish relationships with unbelievers in local neighborhoods."

–DR. ALVIN SANDERS
President/World Impact

"As a former pastor, I saw more people come to Christ through Vacation Bible School than any other ministry at the church. I'm so thankful for VBS and how it had the ability to reach into kids' lives for eternity."

–WILL GRAHAM
Vice President and Associate Evangelist, Billy Graham Evangelistic Association

"VBS is a gift to the spiritual formation and discipleship of the next generations. In our own congregation, Calvario City Church, and our network of congregations at the National Latino Evangelical Coalition have seen the indelible impact that VBS has had in lifting up children and young people who are fully committed to Jesus. VBS is a ministry that is catalytic for the future of the Church in America."

–REV. DR. GABRIEL SALGUERO
President, National Latino Evangelical Coalition and Pastor, Calvario City Church, Orlando, Florida

INTRO AND CHAPTER 1

1. C.H. Spurgeon, *Come Ye Children,* (Scotland: Christian Focus Publications, 1989), 11

2. "Churchgoers Believe in Sharing Faith, Most Never Do," LifeWay Research, August 13, 2012, https://lifewayresearch.com/2012/08/13/churchgoers-believe-in-sharing-faith-most-never-do/

3. "LifeWay VBS Report Forms," 2017

4. "The State of Vacation Bible School," Barna, July 9, 2013, https://www.barna.com/research/the-state-of-vacation-bible-school/#.UfhGxl2siSp

5. "Mobile Kids: The Parent, the Child and the Smartphone," *Nielsen,* 2016 https://www.nielsen.com/us/en/insights/news/2017/mobile-kids--the-parent-the-child-and-the-smartphone.html

6. Aaron Wilson, "Raising lowercase z's," *Facts and Trends*, October, 2017, https://factsandtrends.net/2017/10/11/raising-lowercase-zs/

7. "Cigna U.S. Loneliness Index," May 1, 2018, https://www.multivu.com/players/English/8294451-cigna-us-loneliness-survey/docs/IndexReport_1524069371598-173525450.pdf

8. LifeWay Research, Nothing Less Study, 2016

9. LifeWay Research, It's Worth It Study, 2018

10. Jana Magruder, *Nothing Less,* (Nashville: LifeWay Christian Resources, 2016) 94

11. Phillip Lopate, "The Greatest Year: 1898," *New York Magazine*, January 9, 2011

12. Mary Stuart Smith, "Mrs. Walker Aylett Hawes—A Tribute," *The Richmond Virginian*, April 10, 1916; "A Baptist Deborah," *The Examiner*, October 6, 1904; R.B. Hawes, personal testimonial, Homer Lamar Grice Papers, *Southern Baptist Historical Library and Archives,* Nashville, Tennessee, January, 1942; Alice Broadus Mitchell, personal testimonial, Homer Lamar Grice Papers, *Southern Baptist Historical Library and Archives,* Nashville, Tennessee

13. R.B. Hawes, personal testimonial, Homer Lamar Grice Papers, *Southern Baptist Historical Library and Archives*, Nashville, Tennessee, January, 1942

14. Virginia Hawes, personal notes, Homer Lamar Grice Papers, *Southern Baptist Historical Library and Archives*, Nashville, Tennessee, 1899

15. Mary Stuart Smith, "Mrs. Walker Aylett Hawes—A Tribute," *The Richmond Virginian,* April 10, 1916

16. "How One Woman Saved a Church," *The Christian Herald and Signs of Our Times*, January 16, 1901

17. Steven Gertz, "From Beer to Bibles to VBS," *Christianity Today,* June 2003, https://www.christianitytoday.com/ct/2003/juneweb-only/6-30-43.0.html

18. Mary Stuart Smith, "Mrs. Walker Aylett Hawes—A Tribute," *The Richmond Virginian,* April 10, 1916

19. C.N. Whitney, personal notes, Homer Lamar Grice Papers, *Southern Baptist Historical Library and Archives,* Nashville, Tennessee, 1899

20. Homer L. Grice, "50 Years of Vacation Bible School Work," *The Sunday School Builder*, June, 1951

21. C.N. Whitney, personal notes, Homer Lamar Grice Papers, *Southern Baptist Historical Library and Archives,* Nashville, Tennessee, 1899

22. Virginia Hawes, personal notes, Homer Lamar Grice Papers, *Southern Baptist Historical Library and Archives,* Nashville, Tennessee, 1900

23. Annie M. Burns, personal notes, Homer Lamar Grice Papers, *Southern Baptist Historical Library and Archives,* Nashville, Tennessee, 1900

24. Homer L. Grice, "How Vacation Church Schools Began," *Baptist Leader,* February 1951

25. Homer L. Grice, "Southern Baptists and the Vacation Bible School," *The Quarterly Review,* Second Quarter, 1953

26. Ralph Norman Mould, "Golden Birthday Opportunity," *Baptist Leader,* February 1951

LifeWay Research conducted the *It's Worth It* research for LifeWay Kids. A demographically balanced online panel was used for interviewing American adults. The survey was conducted March 7-10, 2018. Maximum quotas and slight weights were used to balance gender, age, ethnicity, education, and region to more accurately reflect the population. The completed sample of 1,200 surveys provides 95% confidence that the sampling error from the online panel does not exceed +/-3.0 percent. Margins of error are higher in sub-groups.

For surveying children's ministry leaders, LifeWay Research mailed a survey to a random sample of Protestant churches with listed attendance of 50+ (or membership 100+ for those missing attendance) in selected denominations within the following categories: Baptist, Christian/Churches of Christ, Evangelical, Holiness, Independent Fundamentalist, Mennonite, Methodist, and Presbyterian. The survey was conducted June 7—August 8, 2018. Responses were weighted by size and denominational group, including down-weighting an intentional oversample of Southern Baptist churches, to more accurately reflect this population. The sample of 772 surveys provides 95% confidence that the sampling error does not exceed +/-5.6%. (The margin of error accounts for the effect of weighting.) Margins of error are higher in sub-groups.

27. Mary Stuart Smith, "Mrs. Walker Aylett Hawes—A Tribute," *The Richmond Virginian*, April 10, 1916

28. Homer L. Grice, "50 Years of Vacation Bible School Work," *The Sunday School Builder*, June, 1951

29. Porter Routh, "Children Love Vacation Bible School," Homer Lamar Grice Papers, *Southern Baptist Historical Library and Archives*, Nashville, Tennessee, June, 1951

30. Sibley C. Burnett, "The Man Who Put Over 300,000 People To Work," *The Quarterly Review*, Second Quarter, 1953

31. Melita Thomas, "Not Worthy to Walk in His Shoes, A Tribute to Dr. Homer Grice," *LifeWay VBS Blog*, January 27, 2017, https://vbs.lifeway.com/2017/01/27/not-worthy-walk-shoes-tribute-dr-homer-grice/

32. Jerome O. Williams, "Power for the Task," *The Sunday School Builder*, June, 1951

33. "Whatever Happened to Polio?" *Smithsonian National Museum of American History*, https://amhistory.si.edu/polio/americanepi/communities.htm

34. "Church and College Ministry to Children in Daily Vacation Bible Schools," *International Association of Daily Vacation Bible Schools*, 1917

35. Homer L. Grice, *The What-Why-How of the Vacation Bible School*. (The Baptist Sunday School Board, 1942), 32

36. "1900 Looks at 1940," *World Association of Daily Vacation Bible Schools*, January, 1941

37. James L. Sullivan, "The Significance of the Vacation Bible School Movement for the Churches," *The Quarterly Review*, Second Quarter, 1953

38. Andrew Q. Allen, "Why I Have Promoted Vacation Bible School Work," *The Quarterly Review*, Second Quarter, 1953

39. Virginia Hawes, personal notes, Homer Lamar Grice Papers, *Southern Baptist Historical Library and Archives*, Nashville, Tennessee, 1899

40. James L. Sullivan, "The Significance of the Vacation Bible School Movement for the Churches," *The Quarterly Review*, Second Quarter, 1953

CHAPTER 2

1. Timothy and Barbara Frieberg, "Grammar Tags and Lemmas: Analytical Greek New Testament," *UBS4 Greek New Testament with Frieberg Morphology*, 1997

2. "LifeWay VBS Report Forms," 2017

3. "Study Notes," CSB Study Bible, (Nashville: Holman Bible Publishers, 2017) 1553

4. LifeWay Research, It's Worth It Study, 2018

5. LifeWay Research, It's Worth It Study, 2018

6. "LifeWay VBS Report Forms," 2017; "2016 Stats Summary with 2015 Comparison (Rev. Dec, 2017)," United Methodist Church, http://www.gcfa.org/services/data-services/statistical-resources/, 2016; "Church of the Nazarene Growth, 2007-2017," *Annual Statistics from the General Secretary's Reports*, http://www.nazarene.org/sites/default/files/docs/GenSec/Statistics/2017AnnualStatistics.pdf, 2017

7. LifeWay Research, It's Worth It Study, 2018

8. LifeWay Research, It's Worth It Study, 2018

9. Scott Goodson, "Why Brand Building Is Important," *Forbes*, May 27, 2012, https://forbes.com/sites/marketshare/2012/05/27/why-brand-building-is-important/#9a79f1145f72

10. LifeWay Research, It's Worth It Study, 2018

11. Caroline Henderson, "Wanted:Expendable Christians," *The Sunday School Builder*, June, 1951

12. LifeWay Research, It's Worth It Study, 2018

13. LifeWay Research, It's Worth It Study, 2018

14. LifeWay Research, It's Worth It Study, 2018

15. LifeWay Research, It's Worth It Study, 2018

16. LifeWay Research, It's Worth It Study, 2018

17. LifeWay Research, It's Worth It Study, 2018

18. LifeWay Research, It's Worth It Study, 2018

19. LifeWay Research, It's Worth It Study, 2018

20. LifeWay Research, It's Worth It Study, 2018

21. LifeWay Research, It's Worth It Study, 2018

22. LifeWay Research, It's Worth It Study, 2018

23. Mark Moring, "Catching Some Z's," *Facts and Trends*, October, 2017, https://factsandtrends.net/2017/09/29/catching-some-zs/; Dr. Jill Novak, "The Six Living Generations in America," *Marketing Teacher*, http://www.marketingteacher.com/the-six-living-generations-in-america/, 2013, Accessed September 20, 2018

24. Mark Moring, "Catching Some Z's," *Facts and Trends*, October, 2017, https://factsandtrends.net/2017/09/29/catching-some-zs/

25. LifeWay Research, It's Worth It Study, 2018

26. Corrie ten Boom, *In My Father's House* (London: Hodder & Stoughton Ltd, 2005), 94

27. Lonnie Wilkie, "VBS: A Most Effective Evangelism," *Baptist & Reflector,* March 10, 2016, http://baptistandreflector.org/vbs-a-most-effective-evangelism/

28. LifeWay Research, It's Worth It Study, 2018

29. LifeWay Research, It's Worth It Study, 2018

30. LifeWay Research, It's Worth It Study, 2018

31. LifeWay Research, It's Worth It Study, 2018

32. LifeWay Research, It's Worth It Study, 2018

33. "LifeWay VBS Report Forms," 2017

34. J. Howard Williams and J.L. Corzine, "The Vacation Bible School Strengthens State Missions," *The Sunday School Builder*, June, 1951

35. "LifeWay VBS Report Forms," 2017

36. LifeWay Research, It's Worth It Study, 2018

37. LifeWay Research, It's Worth It Study, 2018

38. LifeWay Research, It's Worth It Study, 2018

39. LifeWay Research, It's Worth It Study, 2018

CHAPTER 3

1. "LifeWay VBS Report Forms," 2017

2. LifeWay Research, It's Worth It Study, 2018

3. Mark Moring, "Catching Some Z's," *Facts and Trends*, October, 2017, https://factsandtrends.net/2017/09/29/catching-some-zs/

4. Mark Moring, "Catching Some Z's," *Facts and Trends*, October, 2017, https://factsandtrends.net/2017/09/29/catching-some-zs/

5. LifeWay Research, Nothing Less Study, 2016

6. LifeWay Research, It's Worth It Study, 2018

7. Jana Magruder, *Nothing Less,* (Nashville: LifeWay Christian Resources, 2016) 54

8. LifeWay Research, It's Worth It Study, 2018

9. Jana Magruder, *Nothing Less,* (Nashville: LifeWay Christian Resources, 2016) 59

10. LifeWay Research, It's Worth It Study, 2018

11. Mark Moring, "Catching Some Z's," *Facts and Trends*, October, 2017, https://factsandtrends.net/2017/09/29/catching-some-zs/

12. LifeWay Research, It's Worth It Study, 2018

13. Jana Magruder, Nothing Less, (Nashville: LifeWay Christian Resources, 2016) 49, 94

14. LifeWay Research, It's Worth It Study, 2018

15. LifeWay Research, It's Worth It Study, 2018

16. Jana Magruder, *Nothing Less,* (Nashville: LifeWay Christian Resources, 2017) 80; LifeWay Research, Parenting Study, 2007-08

17. Melita Thomas, "What About VBS," *What About Kids Ministry,* (Nashville: B&H Publishing Group, 2018) 57–58

18. LifeWay Research, It's Worth It Study, 2018

19. LifeWay Research, It's Worth It Study, 2018

CHAPTER 4

1. LifeWay Research, It's Worth It Study, 2018

2. LifeWay Research, It's Worth It Study, 2018

3. LifeWay Research, It's Worth It Study, 2018

4. LifeWay Research, It's Worth It Study, 2018

5. LifeWay Research, It's Worth It Study, 2018

SIDEBARS & INFOGRAPHICS

page 13 "Churchgoers Believe in Sharing Faith, Most Never Do," LifeWay Research, August 13, 2012, https://lifewayresearch.com/2012/08/13/churchgoers-believe-in-sharing-faith-most-never-do/

page 15 "The State of Vacation Bible School," Barna, July 9, 2013, https://www.barna.com/research/the-state-of-vacation-bible-school/#.UfhGxI2siSp

page 16 "Cigna U.S. Loneliness Index," May 1, 2018, https://www.multivu.com/players/English/8294451-cigna-us-loneliness-survey/docs/IndexReport_1524069371598-173525450.pdf

page 19 LifeWay Research, It's Worth It Study, 2018

pages 21–31 Homer L. Grice, "How Vacation Church Schools Began," *Baptist Leader*, February 1951; "Church and College Ministry to Children in Daily Vacation Bible Schools," *International Association of Daily Vacation Bible Schools*, 1917; Willie Beaty, "VBS: An Historic Perspective," *New Horizons in Vacation Bible School*. Nashville, TN: Convention Press, https://s3-us-west-1.amazonaws.com/vbs2016/wp-content/uploads/2018/09/1408O701/History-of-VBS.pdf 1993; Hazel Straight Stafford, *The Vacation Religious Day School*, 1920; "The Student Movement in China," *World Record of Daily Vacation Bible Schools*, 1921; The Standard Vacation Bible School Courses, Standard Publishing, 1923; Porter Routh, "Children Love Vacation Bible School," Homer Lamar Grice Papers, Southern Baptist Historical Library and Archives, Nashville, Tennessee, June, 1951; "1900 Looks at 1940," *World Association of Daily Vacation Bible Schools*, January, 1941; Homer L. Grice,"50 Years of Vacation Bible School Work," *The Sunday School Builder*, June, 1951; Sibley C. Burnett, "The Man Who Put Over 300,000 People To Work," *The Quarterly Review*, 1953; "The Korea Sunday School Association," *The Korea Sunday School Newsletter*, 1931; J.S. Armentrout, "The Daily Vacation Bible School," *The Presbyterian Magazine*, 1932; Ralph Mould, "Golden Birthday Opportunity," *Baptist Leader*, February 1951; "2016 Stats Summary with 2015 Comparison (Rev. Dec, 2017)," United Methodist Church, http://www.gcfa.org/services/data-services/statistical-resources/, 2016; "Church of the

Nazarene Growth, 2007-2017," *Annual Statistics from the General Secretary's Reports,* http://www.nazarene.org/sites/default/files/docs/GenSec/Statistics/2017AnnualStatistics.pdf, 2017

page 22 Photograph courtesy of the Southern Baptist Historical Library and Archives, Nashville, Tennessee

page 23 Virginia Hawes, personal notes, Homer Lamar Grice Papers, *Southern Baptist Historical Library and Archives,* Nashville, Tennessee, 1897

page 25- Photograph courtesy of Southern Baptist Historical Library and Archives, Nashville, Tennessee; Virginia Hawes, personal notes, Homer Lamar Grice Papers, *Southern Baptist Historical Library and Archives,* Nashville, Tennessee, 1898

page 26 Virginia Hawes, personal notes, Homer Lamar Grice Papers, *Southern Baptist Historical Library and Archives,* Nashville, Tennessee

page 27 Homer Lamar Grice Papers, *Southern Baptist Historical Library and Archives,* Nashville, Tennessee

page 36 LifeWay Research, It's Worth It Study, 2018

page 38- Sam Rainer, "Why Vacation Bible School is as Important Now as Ever," July 1, 2018, https://samrainer.com/2018/07/why-vacation-bible-school-is-as-important-now-as-ever/

page 40 LifeWay Research, It's Worth It Study, 2018

page 41 LifeWay Research, It's Worth It Study, 2018

page 42 LifeWay Research, It's Worth It Study, 2018

page 43 LifeWay Research, It's Worth It Study, 2018

page 45 LifeWay Research, It's Worth It Study, 2018

page 47 LifeWay Research, It's Worth It Study, 2018

page 48 LifeWay Research, It's Worth It Study, 2018

page 51 LifeWay Research, It's Worth It Study, 2018

page 52 LifeWay Research, It's Worth It Study, 2018

page 55 LifeWay Research, It's Worth It Study, 2018

page 58 LifeWay Research, It's Worth It Study, 2018

page 60 LifeWay Research, It's Worth It Study, 2018

page 61 LifeWay Research, It's Worth It Study, 2018

page 64 LifeWay Research, It's Worth It Study, 2018

page 65 Lonnie Wilkie, "VBS: A Most Effective Evangelism," *Baptist & Reflector,* March 10, 2016, http://baptistandreflector.org/vbs-a-most-effective-evangelism/

page 67 LifeWay Research, It's Worth It Study, 2018

page 68 LifeWay Research, It's Worth It Study, 2018

page 69 LifeWay Research, It's Worth It Study, 2018

page 71 LifeWay Research, It's Worth It Study, 2018

page 72 "LifeWay VBS Report Forms," 2017

page 75 LifeWay Research, It's Worth It Study, 2018

page 79 LifeWay Research, It's Worth It Study, 2018

page 80 facts and trends article with generations

page 83 LifeWay Research, It's Worth It Study, 2018

page 84 LifeWay Research, It's Worth It Study, 2018

page 85 Nothing Less

page 86 LifeWay Research, It's Worth It Study, 2018

page 87 Bill Emeott, "Leading a Gospel-Centered Kids Ministry," Kids Ministry 101, issue 12; 27

page 89 LifeWay Research, It's Worth It Study, 2018

page 91 Isaiah 55:11

page 93 LifeWay Research, It's Worth It Study, 2018

page 94 LifeWay Research, It's Worth It Study, 2018

page 97 Mark 10:14-16

page 98 LifeWay Research, It's Worth It Study, 2018

page 99 LifeWay Research, It's Worth It Study, 2018

page 100 1 Timothy 4:12

page 101 Jana Magruder, *Nothing Less,* (Nashville: LifeWay Christian Resources, 2017) 80; LifeWay Research, Parenting Study, 2007-08

page 103 LifeWay Research, It's Worth It Study, 2018

page 104 LifeWay Research, It's Worth It Study, 2018

page 107 Melita Thomas, "What About VBS," *What About Kids Ministry,* (Nashville: B&H Publishing Group, 2018) 57–58

page 108 Melita Thomas, "What About VBS," *What About Kids Ministry,* (Nashville: B&H Publishing Group, 2018) 57–58

page 113 LifeWay Research, It's Worth It Study, 2018

page 114 LifeWay Research, It's Worth It Study, 2018

page 117 LifeWay Research, It's Worth It Study, 2018

page 119 LifeWay Research, It's Worth It Study, 2018